5/-

Farewell to Wings

MAURICE FARMAN LONGHORN

Cecil Lewis

FAREWELL TO WINGS

Illustrated by
LEONARD BRIDGMAN

TEMPLE PRESS BOOKS
London · 1964

First published 1964 *by*
TEMPLE PRESS BOOKS LIMITED
42 *Russell Square, London W*C1

© 1964, Cecil Lewis

Printed in Great Britain by
C. TINLING AND CO. LTD.
Liverpool, London and Prescot

Contents

CONTENTS

Foreword

IT IS NOW FIFTY YEARS since the outbreak of the First World War and 49 since, as a gangling boy, I first stepped on the tyre of a Maurice Farman Longhorn, climbing up to the cockpit to become a pilot before I was 18.

This half century has seen astonishing and fearful changes. Technological advances have been so great that the aircraft we flew seem today more remote than the barouche or the warming pan. The very vocabulary, adopted from France, *nacelle, longeron, fuselage, aileron,* has a nostalgic 18th-century ring and, if people could afford it, there is little doubt that an Early Aircraft London to Paris Race would seem as quaint and be as popular as the Veteran Car Rally.

Indeed that very special sort of man, the pilot, is perhaps a dying breed. His courage, his pioneering spirit, his skills are needed less and less. He has outlived his time. The computer, the electronic brain and other remote controls can do his work better and with no fatigue. He is already a 'driver'; soon he will be no more than 'the emergency man', a highly-trained, highly-paid safety precaution whose employers' hope is that they may never need him! In war to send him up to be a target for the homing rocket or the proximity fuse is to doom him to certain death; in peace his real skills are only required for a couple of minutes on take off and landing—all else is, or soon will be, automatic. His exploits are fast becoming legendary and he will soon be enshrined as a curiosity *chez* Madame Tussaud.

Since, although 'sound in wind and limb', I have become, at 66, almost a museum piece myself, it seemed permissible—soon it will be too late—to fill in a corner of history by reminding myself and anyone who thumbs through these pages of the sparkling dawn of life in the air and the way those antiques, the aircraft of the First World War, behaved.

Of us, the pilots of those days, what can I say? We were well paid—it really was danger money—and I suppose inherited from the cavalry a certain dash and style and lived, as someone before me has said (but I cannot remember who), in the 'cynosure of eyes'—that is, the girls ogled us and lured us, sometimes, into those traditional excesses which only youth and war can excuse.

On active service we led an extraordinary double life. Our aerodromes, perhaps 15 miles behind the lines, were near to villages where we lived in comparative comfort in peaceful surroundings. We had sheets, beds and bedding, a good mess, transport to the nearest town and were no more at war once we were 'down' than our parents at home. On the job we were in fact navigating an elementary contraption of spruce and linen with a very low safety factor into areas where it at once became a target for machine-guns and high explosive; a target whose only refuge—naked in the high air—was the skill of the pilot in avoiding (both by aim and accident) being in the place where the guns calculated he would be. We used to reckon we could move 400 yds. between the time an anti-aircraft shell was fired and the moment it burst. This was our period of free manoeuvre and we made a point of using it if the bursts (appearing silently like puff balls in the sky) got close enough to worry us.

But when our duty took us lower to act as eyes for headquarters on the position of our troops, then it was a good deal more uncomfortable. When the battle was going well, the Hun was too busy to bother with us; but when it was not then machine-guns were turned on us to hose us down. It was then a mercy—for concentration on the job and peace of mind—that we had no idea we were being fired at. A great deal of an aeroplane could be holed without affecting its ability to fly. Wings and fuselage could be—and often were— pierced in 50 places, missing the occupants by inches (blissfully unaware of how close it had come until they returned to base). Then the sailmaker would carefully cover each hole with a square inch of Irish linen frayed at the edges and with a brushful of dope make our aircraft 'serviceable' again within an hour. I have had bullets through my engine, bullets through my tanks, bullets through my windscreen and up through the floor of the cockpit between my knees and out over my shoulder and even, on one occasion, had the control stick knocked out of my hand by a splinter of wood chipped off the floorboards by a chance shot—yet never, such is the mystery of destiny, that one bullet which would have been enough to settle my account.

In dogfights the contrasts were even more striking. The concentrated violence of aerial combat has to be experienced to be known, but a hundred pilots in the two wars have brought a stream of testimony to the strain and the jitters that go with it. In my day, though tactics might be worked out beforehand, once off the ground there was no direct communication, other than telepathy. No ground controller with radar directed us towards our 'bandits', no section leader called us on the R.T. to take our man or watch our tails. We may have gone down in formation, but we fought alone and I, personally, had this vivid sense of loneliness in every fight I was in. So a man went into combat as if he were going into death—in extreme danger, and alone.

So, by reason of this strange alternation between war and peace, we lived (as I have said in *Sagittarius Rising*) always in the 'stretch or sag of nerves', being ruthlessly jerked out of the one into the other twice or three times a day. I sometimes think that courage is a material, and expendable, thing of which men are given so much. At first, they use it splendidly, without thought. Then, as they sense the supply getting low, with greater and greater care, growing more and more nervous in the process. For only a fool could come back day after day with the evidence of enemy target practice all over his machine and not be affected by it.

But apart from all this the pilot, viewing the progress of the war on earth from his airy eminence (locked in the noisy silence of his own motor), could not hear the fury of the bombardment, nor the rattle of machine-guns, nor the ragged cheer of the attack; he remained aloft, aloof, lending himself to an event in which he could never really participate. 'Tommy', the marvellous earthbound fighting man, crouched in his trench in mud and filth and went 'over the top' to gain (with wonder at being alive) another trench 50 yards away; but how could such a prospect thrill us who, every time we raised our eyes, could see objective after objective receding for a 100 miles beyond? The horrible futility of war dug deep into our minds and hearts. Never in recorded history had there been such a holocaust as the Somme Battle—hundreds of thousands of young men, the flower of the youth of Europe, the cream of our civilization, died in those summer months. For what? Today we may well question.

Four months after the Armistice in 1918 I celebrated my 21st birthday and began a series of strange ricochets from that first world-shaking tragic explosion which were to take me to the ends of the earth. But now looking back (through years during which it does not seem that the prospect for the human condition, or human hopes, have in any way improved), I seize, like a man finding an antique in the loft, on the carefree gallantry and enthusiasm of those days when the world and I were a lifetime younger and can take you, if you wish, back into the enthusiastic love of flying and flying machines which inspired those years.

Farewell to Wings

1

Maurice Farman
Longhorn

WHENEVER I THINK of the far-away days when I learned to fly at Brooklands, aged 17½, I am reminded of an encounter which I had at a very much later date.

I was a passenger on an aircraft flying from Mexico City to Merida. Just by chance, I found myself sitting next to a very attractive girl. She was quiet and understanding, homely and yet vivacious, and in some way I can't explain, healthy, sound, steady. We had a wonderful conversation. She seemed to like me. I was frankly, suddenly and gloriously infatuated. At Merida we parted. The trip had only lasted a couple of hours. I knew quite well I should never see her again and she must have known it too. We waved to each other casually, 'be seeing you', and that was it. It was only later I began to wake up to what had happened. It was a romance! I should have treasured each moment. She was the most divine creature in the world—and more in the same vein. To be cynical I suppose one could say most of it was exaggerated; but at the time. . . .

My romance with the Maurice Longhorn was just as captivating and wonderful. It only lasted about a couple of hours too—or so my log book tells me. But now, looking back on it after all these years, I feel much as I did about that girl; I didn't appreciate her nearly enough at the time, and only now do I begin to give her true value.

The Maurice Longhorn was the first aeroplane I ever flew in. It was 1915. I had been up to the Air Ministry to be vetted for pilot training and Hugh Cecil, who saw me, doubted whether my six feet four inches could ever be folded into an aeroplane. He sent me down to Hounslow to try. It turned out I could. Then a friendly pilot instructor offered me a flip in a Longhorn and I was airborne for the first time.

A few weeks later I went to Brooklands to be trained as a pilot. I was a 'civil cadet', still wearing mufti. I should not be commissioned till I had proved I could fly. I was the proud possessor of a $2\frac{1}{2}$-h.p. two-stroke Lea Francis motor-bike, the sort you ran alongside and jumped on, and on this I poffered through the gates to the race track, down under the concrete banking and along past the sewage farm to the sheds. Here stood a covey of Maurice Longhorns. You can see they were not, judged by contemporary standards, remarkable for their streamlined beauty; but they were waiting for us and we were wild to get at them—which is, after all, a fair basis for any romance. On closer acquaintance the object of our affections turned out to be free from any vices, and if they weren't very fast, they were extremely reliable and withstood, almost without complaint, quite a lot of knocking about.

That brings up the question of 'rigging'. All our early aeroplanes were 'rigged' and the rigger of those days was a skilled tradesman. His job was to keep the airframe 'trued up'. You can see that the wire bracing of the wing structure was quite complex. Each wire had a turnbuckle at one end. Each of them had to be tightened just the right amount to preserve the shape of the aeroplane. Then each had to be locked into position. When you think there were over a 100 rigging wires in any aircraft you can see the sort of job it was. After a few ropey landings the wires would get stretched. This could affect the 'angle of incidence' of the wings—the thing that makes aeroplanes fly—and if one side had stretched more than another, it could make the machine dangerous in the air. So it would be trundled off to the shed and set up on trestles in an attitude of level flight. Then, after all the wires had been unlocked and slackened off, the job was started with level and plumbob, with templates and protractors, and after about two days' accurate and careful work the machine would be serviceable again.

Although the Longhorn was a sort of aerial joke, like a Daddy Longlegs, it handled beautifully once it was in the air. By far the most difficult thing was to taxi it down-wind to take off. All the struts and wires and the huge box tail, once they were caught by a gust, combined to spin it round nose to wind unless you kept it on the move and anticipated its spins. It was nothing to see young pilots on a gusty day careering off down-wind like Waltzing Matilda. I always heaved a sigh of relief when I could at last let it have its head and swing up into the wind like a kite.

The Longhorn took off at about 40 m.p.h. and didn't do much above 55 m.p.h. full out, so there wasn't a large margin between stop and go—and anyhow with the primitive instruments of those days you flew more by feel than figures. Instruments! What bliss they would be to today's flight engineer! There were three of them: a Rev. Counter which usually seemed to have a faulty drive and a needle that wandered jauntily between 200 r.p.m. above and below normal revs; a Bubble, not unlike a carpenter's level except that the tube was curved and showed you—if the bubble was central—that you were not sideslipping; and a sort of Thermos flask with a red column of liquid which rose and fell with its speed. This was called the Pitôt Tube and worked off the Pitôt Head. Both Pitôt Head and Bubble were in use up to the end of the war. Actually with the Longhorn no instruments were really necessary. You could tell your speed by the sound of the singing wires. You could feel the wind on the side of your face if you sideslipped. You could hear the note of the engine fall if you lost revs. Seated in the little slipper set on the lower plane, your rudder, elevator and aileron controls were large and simple. In fact the 'spectacle' type of control column then fitted to the Longhorn is still modern practice today, 50 years later. Out ahead were the great skids with the elevator between them, a nice cushion if you *did* happen to make a bad landing. The 70-h.p. Renault was

3

reliable. The four wheels were held over the skids in pairs by yards and yards of rubber, muscle-developer, cord. They took up the shocks of bad landings in a wonderful way. They had to.

It speaks well for the simplicity—and strength—of the dear old Longhorn that I was sent off solo after 1 hour 25 minutes' dual, and that I returned the aeroplane on that occasion—and every other—in one piece.

2

Maurice Farman Shorthorn

FIRST SOLO is a turning point in every pilot's career. Depending on how long he takes to get to it he can be roughly classed as to his natural flying aptitude. In the Second World War I did 1,000 hours *ab initio* training—teaching young men to fly. Those with real skill could be got away solo in a little over seven hours. The good average pilot would be away before 10 hours' dual. From 12 to 15 hours came the doubtful ones who (strange as it may seem) were allotted to Transport Command. Those who could not go solo in 15 hours were fired. As an instructor myself I found these figures very interesting. I taught my own son to fly—I think it is the only case in the R.A.F.—and though he had great natural aptitude I couldn't get him off solo in under seven hours.

How then was it possible for young men in 1915 to go solo, as I did, with anything from an hour and a half to two hours' dual? I really don't think the aeroplanes were any easier to fly or any easier to land. I can't imagine that we were such wonderful chaps that we could do things in a quarter of the time our sons could! The thing remains a mystery. I can only testify that it was so.

Once over the hurdle of first solo, it was obviously necessary to gain experience. To do this we were encouraged to 'put in time' as much as we could. But in 1915 owing to the poor winter weather and the shortage of machines, it was a slow business. The aeroplane on which we tried to gain experience was a sister to the Longhorn called the Shorthorn. This different name was due to the fact that the 'horn' of the Longhorn—that is the great skids and elevator—had been chopped off and the elevator had been transferred to a flap at the back end of the tail. The long skids had been cut back to stumps, the longerons had been pinched together to hold a single tail plane instead of the box; but the whole of the rest of the aeroplane was more or less unchanged.

As you can see from the drawings these alterations made the Shorthorn into quite a workmanlike job. It had an even better forward and downward view than its sister and when you sat in the front seat you were really in a commanding position for both flying itself and for all the other jobs a pilot was required to do on active service in those days. In fact I was not surprised, some months later, to find the French using squadrons of Maurice Shorthorns in the Somme Battle area. Strengthened up and fitted with a larger engine to give them a bit more speed, they were ideal for reconnaissance and photography and lasted on active service right through the Somme Battle until the autumn of 1916.

I only put in two or three hours on a Shorthorn and that only in circuits round Brooklands—for the idea of learning to do a 'cross country' and landing at another aerodrome was, in those days, quite unheard of. I grew really fond of the Shorthorn. Although when I moved on to Gosport, to fly 'tractors', it was supposed to be a big step forward, I always had a hankering after the pusher type of aeroplane. Perhaps that was why the F.E. 2b had such an appeal for me.

It is extraordinary, looking back on it, to think how rapidly one acquired assurance as a pilot. Once over the crisis of first solo, it began to be easy. There are only two things in flying that are dangerous and difficult. The first is take off and the second landing. In take off the danger does not so much lie in the pilot's lack of skill (although this may sometimes play a part), but in the fear of engine failure when the aircraft is near the ground. How many pilots have been killed by trying to turn back to the aerodrome when their engine failed just after take off! It is nearly always fatal. The only thing to do is to carry straight on and land as best you can. If you tried to turn, particularly in those days of low engine power when stalling was a real danger, it was almost inevitable that a wing would drop and the aeroplane would just nosedive into the ground. The tension every pilot feels on take off was accentuated at Brooklands by the saucer-shaped concrete racing track which, though it only rose perhaps 50 ft. into the air, seemed a terrible hazard to us. What a place it was, come to think of it, to teach young men to fly! We were always afraid of hitting the edge of the track (some pilots did) and going arsy-tarsy down the other side. Certainly it vetoed any idea, if our engine failed, of turning back into the field. But once a pilot had sufficient confidence to know that his machine would easily clear the track this hazard ceased to be so frightening. Returning to the aerodrome and landing required skill of quite a different order. Engine failure on take off was a hazard a pilot couldn't do much about, but bad landings were in 99 cases out of 100 just lack of judgement and skill.

It must be remembered that the pioneer pilot of 1915 had absolutely no instruments to help him. Even the technique of pilot training (which was developed in the Second World War into quite a science) did not really exist. We had to pick up the characteristics of each new aeroplane we flew and write our own handling notes. Naturally young pilots did not take any liberties with their machines, but the modern technique of 'motoring' in on about a quarter throttle was then quite unknown and would have been frowned on by all of us because, if your engine cut, such an approach would land you in trouble. Nowadays when engines are 100 per cent reliable and multi-engine aircraft are the order of the day all these techniques are different. But if engines were unreliable and characteristics different, aeroplanes in those days were small and easily manoeuvrable. The techniques adopted, therefore, were to get pretty close to the down-wind side of the airfield, cut the motor and then lose height in a set of vertical turns, coupled with a good sideslip. In this way it was quite possible to lose 500 ft. very quickly and then just level up and put her down.

Needless to add, since no form of radio control existed, a pilot, once he was airborne, was on his own and there were no means of warning him if another machine happened to be landing at the same time as he was. But here again the early days had another advantage: runways were unknown. There was simply a nice large grass field and if you saw another chap coming in to land at the same time as you, well, there would be plenty of room for him at one side of the field while you put down on the other.

B.E. 2c

DURING NINETEEN SIXTEEN the aeroplane most frequently seen up and down the Western Front in the British Sector was the B.E. 2c. It was a sort of maid of all work, a general purpose hack, which could be used for reconnaissance, artillery observation, photography, spy dropping or any other job that turned up. When I think of it, I categorize it as the 'normal' form of biplane tractor. It had been developed (if you are a fan for those things) from the B.E. 2a and 2b. A certain amount of cowling and streamlining had rounded it out. The dihedral of the main planes (then new) made it what was called 'inherently stable', which meant it would straighten itself up after a turn, rather like castoring action on a car. It was steady, reliable, easy to handle and though, from a pilot's point of view, it left lots to be desired, it was the best thing going at the time and the mainstay of the routine work of the R.F.C. during those crucial days of the war.

The B.E. 2c was the first tractor I ever flew. Coming on from Brooklands to Gosport (in a brand new double-breasted tunic and ready-made field boots which gave me corns), my only experience was of 'pushers'. Whatever the shortcomings of the old Maurice Farman, you could at least see where you were going. The 'tractor' seemed, at first, a dreadful handicap (indeed it was). There in front of you was a second cockpit, where your instructor (and later your observer) sat. Then there were tanks, then there was an engine. So you couldn't see ahead at all, you could only lean over and look out one side or another. But quite apart from that there were the lower planes thoroughly obstructing the view forwards and downwards. There were the upper planes cutting out a large section of the air above. In fact a biplane tractor was a very poor piece of apparatus for a pilot to see out of. On patrol the observer spent most of the time kneeling on his seat and keeping a sharp look-out over the tail—and getting bloody cold in the process.

I didn't do much work on the B.E. 2c. But I have two vivid memories of the aeroplane. The first was early in 1916 when I had just been posted to a '2c' Squadron (No. 9). After a few hours pottering about 'putting in time' getting to know the sector, getting the hang of the French maps and so on, I was sent out to take a set of photos of the front line trenches. With me was a Sergeant Observer, who didn't much relish the job—and small blame to him, for fledgling pilots, just out from home, had too often meant death in the afternoon for chaps like him.

We had nothing to do really that day except keep a sharp eye open for enemy attack (and he did it jolly well). I had to take the photographs for the simple reason that the pilot's cockpit was behind the planes and the camera could only look down from there.

For, of course, the camera was not a 'fitting'. It was slung on the side of the fuselage outside, and it was a real old studio model, complete with leather concertina, mahogany frame and boxes of plates—yes, plates! There was a sort of rudimentary 'ring and ball' sight to give you some idea of what you were taking—as you leaned out into a 70-m.p.h. wind and tried to see through the sight without getting your goggles blown off. To take a photo you grabbed at a ring on the end of a bit of wire, which was skittering about in the gale, and to change the plates there was a sort of mahogany knife handle which you pushed steadily forward and then pulled back. This was at the back of the polished cigar box full of 24 plates. From this Emmet-like contraption we produced

10

hundreds of excellent photographs, greatly to the liking of the Intelligence Section of the 3rd and 15th Army Corps.

It was a beautiful April afternoon and the earth looked lovely in the dazzle of spring. The entire sector of the lines lay—as it seemed from 8,000 ft.— peaceful and deserted. We took our bearings from Albert and moved off towards the Front near Montauban, put ourselves squarely over the lines and started taking the photos. This meant flying the old B.E. and keeping on course with the left hand, operating the camera with the right, and leaving the sergeant observer kneeling on the front seat to keep a smart look-out for Fokkers.

All went well till we'd pretty well emptied the box of 24 plates. We were at No. 22 when our peace was interrupted by a couple of innocent-looking black smoke puffs right ahead of the nose and about 100 ft. below. They were followed by two more dead underneath and close enough for me to smell the cordite. 'Ess! Ess!' yelled the sergeant over the engine and the wind. 'They've ranged us!'

Obediently I 'essed' and after a few moments the Ack-ack shells were bursting a quarter of a mile away. But the bursts had drawn the attention of a roving Fokker to our existence, and no sooner were we back on course getting our last two photos when the sergeant, now stiffened like a pointer in his seat, yelled 'Fokker!' and I turned my head to see the fine slim line of the Hun monoplane rapidly coming up behind.

I managed to get the last photo just before he opened fire and then heard, as if muffled and far away, the sound of a machine-gun. He was firing at us. A second later the sergeant's gun was clattering and spewing 'empties', a hole appeared in the windscreen just to the right of my head, then the sergeant's gun jammed and the engine set up a terrible clatter. It all happened at once and I certainly did not stand on the order of my going. The sergeant was yelling: 'Jammed! Jammed! My gun's jammed!' I had cut the throttle and put the old 2c into a steep left-hand dive. The Fokker (luckily) didn't follow. The sergeant was scanning the sky, furiously pulling on the breach of the Lewis gun.

I was making for the emergency forward landing ground. There was a wonderful sense of relief.

We made the ground and landed, jumped out, examined the holes in the machine made by the Fokker. It was wonderful to be down. There was the ground solid underfoot, the warm blue sky above. The sergeant congratulated me on my narrow escape. Six inches to the right of my head a bullet had gone through the windscreen. We pulled over the engine and diagnosed a cracked piston or connecting rod, phoned the Squadron and, after putting a guard on the machine and getting the photos off to the Corps, got a lift back. It had been quite an afternoon!

My other sharp memory is of one of those idiotic experiences in which I just made a fool of myself. It was 1918. I had to ferry a 2c from Southend round to Hounslow. It was a joyride, which meant a night in town on the way back; but it was also a November afternoon and very foggy. I had to make a circuit of London (to avoid the barrage balloons) and somewhere between Brooklands and Hounslow I got lost. By this time I was down to a few hundred feet and the fog was thickening up with evening. I decided to come down in the first decent field and ask where I was.

I found a nice flat field, landed, and got my bearings from a butcher's boy—I was almost at Hounslow—and then the fun began. I had to start the engine and get back into the cockpit. It sounds quite easy. But . . . first I had to go to the cockpit, set the throttle, make sure the switch was off, then walk round to the front and turn the engine over to get mixture into the cylinders. I was dressed in long sheepskin flying boots up to my thighs, a fur-lined leather jacket, fur helmet and heavy fur gauntlet gloves. Having 'sucked in' I went back to set the throttle and switch on the engine. Then I walked back to the nose and swung the propeller. When the engine started, I would go back to the cockpit.

It was all quite simple and worked according to plan, except that when the engine started it turned out that I had set the throttle a bit above idling speed. It ran fast enough to set the aircraft moving. In fact it was running too fast for me to get round the plane and back to the cockpit to pull the throttle closed. All I could do was grab the wing tip and hold on. This put the rudder hard over and started the 2c turning in a fairly small circle. Problem—how to get back to the cockpit?

I soon had to let go the wing tip and move smartly out of the circle. The B.E., like a slightly irritated hornet, continued to circle, working itself slowly over towards the hedge. By now, having warmed up a little, it was running faster and, heavily dressed as I was, I couldn't sprint fast enough to dash in as it came round and make the pilot's seat. I tried it twice, fell flat on my face and got caught by the wheels on the next circuit. By this time I was sweating and furious. But I had to give it up and after a quarter of an hour the B.E. quietly crunched into the hedge, broke the prop, tore the wing tips and stopped.

Moral: never start an aeroplane if you're not in the cockpit.

4

Avro 504

MY FIRST ENCOUNTER with this famous trainer was also at Gosport. I had come on from Brooklands with about three hours' solo in my log book. Now I was to fly 'modern' machines in an 'advanced training' programme.

After the B.E. 2c the next step was the Avro and introduction to rotary engines. As a boy of $17\frac{1}{2}$, I was avid for every new experience of flying. In those days aeroplanes were simple mechanisms. No special training programme was necessary to familiarize pilots with new types. So my instructor and I 'looked over' the Avro one afternoon before having a flip together.

The characteristic of the Avro—by which you could tell it a mile off—was a little skid, not unlike a ski, in the centre of the axle carrying the wheels of the undercarriage. This skid was presumably to protect the propeller if the machine was landed with its tail too high or to prevent it doing a ground loop perhaps; but during the war I saw hundreds of Avros, and never heard of one being saved by the skid—or indeed damaging it. It was just one of those excrescences, like the human tail, which may have been useful once, but has long ago ceased to function. But the Avro's skid was its trademark. I doubt if we should have recognized it without one.

Apart from this it was a very straightforward and well designed aeroplane. Handy on the controls, simple to fly, with no vices or idiosyncracies. The only thing that intimidated the novice was its rotary engine. It was the French designers who had developed the 'rotary'. First there was the Gnôme, then the Monosoupape (a larger Gnôme), then came the Le Rhône (made in two sizes, 80 h.p. and 100 h.p.), and later the Clerget which remained in service right up to the end of the war.

I don't know who first hit upon the idea of an engine in which the crankshaft was fixed and the cylinders spun round it, but this starfish arrangement had certain advantages in engines of low power. But when more power was wanted and it was soon superseded by the normal radial engine: the rotary is now as extinct as the dodo.

However, from the pilot's point of view, the whole technique of handling an aircraft fitted with a rotary, either on the ground or in the air, was quite different—for the simple reason that these engines had only two possibilities: they were either 'On', and running full bore, or they were 'Off'. Later, rotaries like the Le Rhône and the Clerget were developed that worked on a somewhat different principle. They had a carburetter and two valves. They could be throttled back to a certain extent; but the old Avro with its 100-h.p. Mono was in use long before this refinement.

So the 'vital actions' in the cockpit were simple. You turned on the petrol and opened a 'throttle' needle valve which supplied juice to the crankcase. The mechanic then 'sucked in', that is to say, he spun the propeller, so that petrol vapour would pass up through ports in the cylinder wall into the cylinders and there combine with air drawn in through a little suction valve on the cylinder head. This valve was uncontrolled and just sucked air as long as the piston moved down. The resultant mixture was explosive *only* if the correct amount of vapour had got into the cylinder—and everything was designed for this to work only when the motor ran full out. So, after 'sucking in' till most of the cylinders were full of mixture, the mechanic called 'Contact!' The pilot switched on, the mechanic heaved on the propeller, there was a roar as the engine caught and you were *immediately* ready to take off!

But as this was usually impossible straight off the tarmac, it was necessary to taxi. To do this the engine had constantly to be switched on and off and indeed a bellpush, or button switch, had been carefully fixed on the top of the mahogany joystick for this very purpose. So no sooner had the engine 'caught' than you 'pressed the tit', as we used to say, and stopped it again and then kept bursting it 'Brr-rp! Brr-rp!' as you waved away the chocks. Put the rudder hard over: Brr-rp Brr-rp, and the tail was thrown round. Reverse rudder: Brr-rp Brr-rp, and it was straight again. So in a series of Brr-rps you proceeded down wind, swung round, took your finger off the button and let her go!

How glorious it seems in retrospect! The simplicity and enthusiasm that then surrounded flying and the men who flew. Toffed up in our leather coats and knee-high flying boots, leather helmets, goggles and fur-lined chin pieces for the winter, we looked like the popular idea of 'the men from Mars'. But in summer I often flew without coat, helmet or goggles. In fact, in 1918 I tested a new machine up to 20,000 ft. dressed just as I had come out of the mess— and, of course, without any oxygen. My reactions may have been affected, but, if, so, I was unaware of it.

But to return to the Avro, everything was fine while it was fine; but if, for instance, the flex connecting the button switch broke, then there was no way to stop the engine except by turning off the petrol or cutting the main switch. Everybody got so used to the button switch it was easy to forget that other means of stopping the engine existed—besides, the button switches rarely, if ever, packed up.

However, mine packed up on my very first solo! I had just come down, landed and was taxiing in, very pleased with myself. There were a lot of aircraft on the tarmac including several new F.E. 2b's. Suddenly the button switch didn't answer. The engine roared out and I couldn't stop it. I was aimed straight at the sheds and all those aeroplanes! Anyone with a bit of experience would have snapped off the main switch at once. But for the novice down from his first solo, that was too much to expect. I jammed on full rudder. Round flew the tail. I was paralysed. I hadn't the sense to take off again, cool down and remember the other controls. I just sat hypnotized while the Avro spun round and round in a tight circle, working nearer and nearer to all those other aircraft with every turn. Suddenly, when disaster was imminent, the engine, for no reason, coughed and stopped.

My instructor leapt at me like a madman. 'What the bloody . . . hell are you up to? You lunatic!' And more in the same strain. I explained. We cooled off. There was no damage to H.M. property and only a burst tyre to the Avro. But I'd got the message: Never trust a button switch!

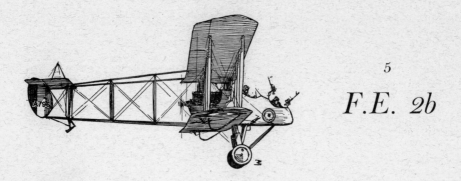

5

F.E. 2b

I WELL REMEMBER the first time I ever saw an F.E. 2b. It was January, 1916. No. 23 Squadron was being equipped with them and would shortly take off for France. As I had been detailed to proceed overseas as spare pilot for the next squadron, I was pretty interested to see what the F.E. 2b looked like.

Drawings (or even a model) give little idea of the most striking thing about this aeroplane, which was its famous 'oleo' undercart. I suppose this was the first time that telescopic oil buffers had ever been used to absorb landing shocks. The thing worked all right; but in the air the two legs hung down, fully extended, in a very limp and gawky manner—looking as if they were tied on to the rest of the structure with string and might, at any moment, fall off.

On landing, while the F.E. 2b was still six feet up, the wheels touched the ground with a long chattering rumble and as the weight of the aircraft came down on them they gradually telescoped and took up the strain. It was almost impossible to make a bad landing with an F.E. 2b, so beautifully did those giraffe-like legs cushion and touch down. Once fully compressed, the aircraft looked quite normal.

As you can see from the drawing, the F.E. 2b was a 'pusher'. Its engine was situated behind the wings and the propeller behind that. The great virtue of this arrangement (now quite obsolete) was the splendid forward arc of observation and fire it gave the crew. In the nacelle, shaped like an old boot, the pilot sat fairly high up in the heel and the observer squatted down in the toe. Ahead, he had a formidable arc of fire while the pilot had a tube sticking up on each side of his cockpit into which he could stick the spigot mounting of a Lewis gun. His mountings were so placed that he could—provided he was able to fly the aircraft with his knees—turn half round in his seat and fire his gun backwards over the top plane behind him.

The 'Supremacy of the Air' was every bit as important to us in 1916 as it was in the Battle of Britain—only 24 years later. In the early spring of 1916 we did not have this supremacy and squadrons which had to work beyond the enemy front line were pretty sensitive about meeting the famous Fokker which had become a legend and whose attacks were dreaded all along the Western Front. So the question of fire power and, in particular, the ability to protect your own tail was very important to us all.

However, it turned out that a group of F.E. 2b's in formation was pretty well invulnerable. When attacked they used to form a circle and flying round and round were able to protect each other's tails and produce a dangerous concentration of fire if attacked head on. The circle gradually edged its way back over the lines to safety, although the Hun had usually given up the attack long before then. The F.E. 2b was designed and built by the Royal Aircraft Factory, Farnborough. As pilots, we didn't think much of the R.A.F.* designs, they weren't as stylish as some of the private firms producing aircraft at that time, but we had to admit that they were usually pretty solid-looking jobs. The F.E. 2b was no exception. Its copper-jacketed Beardmore engine of 120 h.p. was wonderfully reliable and the 'fitters'—as the engine mechanics of those days were called—were very proud of these engines. They used to polish up the copper till you could see your face in it. As the engine was water cooled and heavy, it was somewhat difficult to start it by heaving the propeller round (the

* When the Royal Air Force was formed, the Royal Aircraft Factory changed its name to the Royal Aircraft Establishment.

way nearly all aeroplanes were started up in those days). So the F.E. had another novel gadget. This consisted of a starter magneto, a little dynamo in the cockpit with a handle which, when you spun it, caused a spark at the plugs and, with luck, would set the engine rolling.

Gradually No. 23 Squadron gathered its aircraft until all 12 arrived and the three flights of four each were readied to take off for France. Although I had only done about 10 hours' solo at that time I was bitterly disappointed not to be going with them (I had to follow on with the men by boat to Rouen). So it was that I stood on the tarmac at Gosport and watched the Squadron take off for France. Each aircraft came lumbering up, the noise of its engine growing to a climax till it crashed past overhead, the sound rapidly fading behind the sheds. The 12 aircraft, slowly circling the field, formed up in three diamond flights and headed off for Dover and the Channel to begin their operational life overseas. Later the F.E. 2b was improved with a larger engine and various other modifications, but, like all aircraft, it eventually became outclassed by the faster and more manoeuvrable types of 'tractor'-engined machines. Still, all those who flew the 'pushers' of the old days will never forget the good feeling they gave of really being able to see where you were going. But, of course, once twin-engined aircraft became general, the cockpit got back its 'pusher' view and has never lost it since.

6

B.E. 12

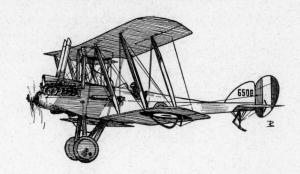

I ONLY FLEW the B.E. 12 once and that was pure coincidence. As spare pilot to 23 Squadron, I got as far as Rouen with the men. But then they caught up with me. Pilots were in short supply and no squadron could carry 'spares'. So I got posted to No. 9 Squadron flying B.E. 2c's. The C.O. was furious at being sent an allegedly fully operational pilot with only 13 hours 25 minutes' flying to his credit. Murder! he called it. So he started giving me jobs flying here and there to 'put in time'. But when he had to give up a pilot for training on Moranes—a death trap all pilots avoided—he sent me, since I was more or less useless to him.

So I arrived at St. Omer and began to learn to fly the famous Morane Parasol. When I had managed to flop around in it a few times and bring it back all in one piece, a bit of luck came my way. They wanted a Parasol for training back in Gosport—and I got the job of taking one home to 'Blighty'. (When we went overseas in those days, we didn't dream of seeing the old country again in under six to nine months, so to get back to see the girl friend in just a few weeks was bliss.)

It was an absolutely stinking day, clouds right down on the deck. High wind. But who cares when the destination is home. I picked my way along the roads at roof-top height till I got to the coast, launched out over the Channel at 100 ft., hit the south coast somewhere—I didn't know where except that I had to do a sharp left turn to avoid the cliffs—and tooled along westwards in the direction of Gosport. After all I had only to hug the coast and I was bound to get there. But the weather got worse, the rain poured down. I couldn't see anything. It was late afternoon and I suddenly thought it would really be far better to be safely down on the deck. So when I suddenly saw an aerodrome, I landed. It was Shoreham.

The next train to London was the order of the day. I returned the morning after and took the Morane on to Gosport. Then I was told to report to Farnborough to ferry a machine back to France. I got to Farnborough where they told me the aircraft would not be ready till the next day. My mother was working at a hospital near Haslemere, so I borrowed a motorbike from a trustful despatch rider and set off for the cottage at Hindhead. Mother was not expecting me and thinking secretly, I suppose, that she would never see her only son again—for the life of a pilot on the Western Front in 1916 was three weeks— she burst into tears, so close are joy and sorrow. We had a wonderful brief time together. Then I chugged back to Farnborough.

It was only then I learned I was to ferry a B.E. 12 back to France. I had never heard of the thing; but every new aeroplane was an excitement and a challenge so I examined my 'mount' with interest. It was really nothing but a higher-powered single-seater B.E. 2c armed with a forward-firing Vickers gun. The front seat had been taken out to make room for the new 140-h.p. R.A.F. engine. For those days this engine looked huge. It was air cooled and (as far as I remember) had 12 cylinders inclined in a narrow vee. This extra length, plus extra tanks, filled up the whole of the forepart of the fuselage. The pilot's cockpit was normal, aft of the wings as in the B.E. 2c. With the increased power and bigger tanks the B.E. 12 was intended for long-range photography, occasional bomb raids and even to fight the Fokker. But it was really a washout— not fast or manoeuvrable enough for any duties and 'Boom' Trenchard soon had it out of service.

It really was a cow. The engine gave full revs and full power while sounding as if there was something radically wrong with it. The big four-bladed pro-peller seemed to increase the vibration. It was a lovely day and I crossed the Channel high up, glad of the height, for full out or throttled back the engine rattled like a can of old nails. I was glad enough to put it down at the depot, saying fervently to the group of pilots who gathered round the newcomer, 'You can have it. That's one I don't want to see again.'

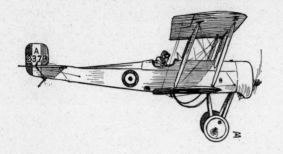

7

Bristol
Scout

THE BRISTOL SCOUT was a single-seater biplane, so small that even an average man had to be eased in with a shoehorn. A man of my size ought never to have been allowed to get in; but my ambition had always been for 'scouts' and there it stood on the St. Omer aerodrome. Patrick, my instructor, didn't seem to object. So I wedged myself into the cockpit. It was so narrow that my knees prevented any lateral movement of the stick. So short that I could hardly move the rudder. I had done about 15 hours' flying and this was the first single-seater I had ever sat in.

Of course it was frightfully exciting and my heart was beating with pride and excitement as I taxied out for take-off. The 80-h.p. Gnôme was controlled, just like the old Avro, with a button switch in the joystick head and I flipped the engine on and off as I swung off downwind. It was such a small aeroplane, so light, so sensitive; it would be wonderful in the air!

So I swung into wind, let the engine go and managed to take off all right. Once aloft it was easy and I gingerly tried out mild turns and stalls to get the feel of the machine. I wanted to 'stunt' it, of course. All pilots in those days—so it seems to me looking back—were wild exhibitionists. All we wanted to do was show off. All the same, the machine was really too small for me and I knew I hadn't sufficient freedom of movement on the controls.

Besides it was only yesterday I had done my first loop—and that had been quite a landmark in my flying career. I had mentioned it as casually as I could to Patrick.

'I'm going to loop,' I said to Patrick, much as a man might announce he was going over Niagara Falls in a bath-tub.

'Oh!' he said, quite unconcerned. He was busy with a compass. I walked away, rather huffed. He might encourage a chap. Apparently he woke up to the fact that something more was expected of him. He called after me: 'Hey! Plenty of speed! Put her well up to a hundred! And remember, when you cut off your engine at the top you'll need some right rudder to counteract the torque. Otherwise you'll fall out of it sideways. If you come out square the first time, I'll stand you a drink—a couple of drinks,' he added, as an afterthought.

I took off and climbed to 3,000 ft. Then I put the nose down. How she screamed, diving with the engine full out! Eighty-five, ninety, ninety-five . . . She was screaming and vibrating like hell. I lost my nerve. I wouldn't try it. I hadn't intended to do it. I was only seeing what it felt like to go fast with the engine on. After all, I hadn't got to do the beastly stunt. It was no earthly use, anyway. I'd do it tomorrow, when the machine had been trued up and didn't vibrate so. I'd . . . But, of course, old Pat would be watching. How could I come down and face him? 'Lost your nerve?' he would inquire, and I should go down, right bang to the bottom, in his estimation. Well . . . I'd have another try. Throttle full open. Eighty-five, ninety, ninety-five . . . She's not shaking quite so much . . . a hundred . . . a hundred and five . . . Now! I pulled back the stick. The horizon disappeared. Everything was sky. Up and up I went. I must be over now, I thought. But there was nothing. I hung on to the stick, looking upwards. At last, there, right above me, was the rim of the horizon! I was over! Engine off! The 2c came shooting down on the dive, I kept the stick back, and gradually the speed fell off. I'd done it! And what's more, I'd remembered the rudder and come out straight—or I thought I had. Pat would owe me a drink—a couple of drinks.

By this time I was down to 1,000 ft. I opened the throttle to get the right side of the aerodrome to come in. Nothing happened. I shut it and opened it again. Not a splutter. Plenty of pressure in the tank. Try the gravity. Quick, switch over! No good. Not a cough. This means a forced landing. I must have oiled the plugs up at the top of the loop. Damn! I can't get back to the aerodrome. Where's the wind? I've only got 500 ft. This ploughed field will have to do. This would happen just when I've looped. Hell! Here goes! And I settled her down into the furrows of the plough without accident. My first loop and my first forced landing all in one. I sat there in the middle of the field, cooling off, for both those things had required the limit of my skill and nerve at that time. Soon a tender came down the road. In it were Patrick and a couple of mechanics. I was out of the machine, examining the engine.

'What's the matter?' shouted Pat as he came up.

'She cut out, after the loop. I must have oiled the plugs up.'

'Funny!' He walked round to the cockpit. 'Did you switch off on the top of that loop? It was a good one, by the way.'

The horrible truth dawned on me. 'Why, yes, I suppose I did. You told me to.'

'I said, cut your engine off. With the throttle, not the switch, you lunatic. You never switched on again, did you?' He laughed. 'You're a damn fine pilot! Contact!' The mechanic had been spinning the prop. Now he gave a sharp jerk and away she went. 'Fancy fetching me all the way out here for that! You forfeit those drinks. They're on you, my boy. Jump up, I'll flip you back.' We popped over the hill and down on to the aerodrome.

'Actually, you didn't do so badly,' said Pat, as we walked into the bar. 'You didn't smash the machine up, and that's more than a lot of chaps could say on their first forced landing. And the loop was a beauty. I'll stand you a gin, after all.'

No doubt it was because of yesterday that Patrick had trusted me with the Bullet. I mustn't let him down. I flew about for 20 minutes or so and returned to the aerodrome to land. The wind had shifted and these light machines were very sensitive to being brought in out of wind. As I held her off I saw my drift and this panicked me. I was too high anyway and jabbed nervously at the rudder to get her to swing into wind. She didn't answer. There was a big bounce, then another, the undercarriage vee-struts collapsed and over she went on her back.

I scrambled out, unhurt; but terribly ashamed and crestfallen. Pilots strolled up to examine the damage, which luckily wasn't bad. Patrick was caustic. I felt awful. But some good may have come of it, for, partly by wonderful luck no doubt, that was the only time in the whole of my flying days that I ever bent an aeroplane.

8
Morane Parasol

IT CERTAINLY wasn't love at first sight, or second or third; but I did eventually come to a respect and affection for the old Parasol that I never had for any other aeroplane. I even thought her beautiful and spent hours devising ways to streamline her wires, to beautify her nose and deciding what colour to dope the linen spoke covers of her two wire wheels.

In the Parasol I did my longest stint at the front—seven months on the Somme in 1916. In her I did my best work in the war, for which I was twice mentioned in despatches and awarded the Military Cross. From under the shadow of her wings I saw sights that changed me in a few short months from a callow boy to a disillusioned young man. She was ropey, treacherous, dangerous to fly, permitted no liberties and needed attention every second she was in the air. But only once on 200 patrols did she ever let me down.

You can see what this paragon was like to look at; but you can have no idea what she was like to fly. 'Good' design implies flying characteristics that more or less automatically ensure that an aircraft flies straight and level hands off. In that case the Parasol was a thoroughly bad design, for she had only one position to which she automatically reverted and that was a vertical nosedive. The reason for this was simple: she had no tail. She had only a pair of 'balanced' elevators (with about one-third of their area ahead of the fulcrum). These were

MORANE PARASOL

terribly sensitive and the instant you took your hand off the stick, flicked over. The stick cracked forward, clank!—into the oil tank, the machine immediately stood on its nose and you had a fine and sudden view of the earth directly below. You grabbed the stick rather hurriedly and pulled it back, whereupon it flicked into the opposite position and the old Parasol stood blithely on its tail! Between these two extremes was a balance you had to find to hold the machine straight and level. The Parasol was no machine to doze in.

By contrast the rudder was too small and sluggish in action, while the ailerons hardly worked at all. Time and time again, taking off over the sheds in the boisterous westerly wind, the Parasol would put a wing down and extreme opposite stick had no effect whatever. You sat there, holding on, stick hard over, and just waited, praying the wing tip would miss the tops of the sheds. Usually about a quarter of a mile further on, the wing would condescend slowly to come up again. This uncontrollability was a menace: it was also a challenge and certainly a situation in which to cultivate accurate flying and keep wide awake. Only two squadrons in the R.F.C. were equipped with Parasols—Nos. 1 and 3. Though they were reputed by all to be death traps, they were docile and cosy once you knew the drill, but we were always on guard. It was a squadron rule never to turn the machine under 500 ft.

Operationally the great virtue in the Parasol lay in the fact that its one wing was above the body, affording the pilot and observer an uninterrupted view downwards. This was perfect for contact patrol—in which we kept close liaison with front-line troops in the attack—and also for artillery observation and general ground reconnaissance. Sitting snugly in front, warmed by the engine, the pilot's little bucket seat was set low in the ample fuselage. The observer just behind him was close enough to shout into his ear. (We did not have to shut off the engine like the 2c's did when we wanted to tell our mates something!)

The only occasion when the Parasol packed up on me was one morning on the dawn patrol shortly after the Somme offensive had begun. We were air-borne at 4 a.m. and an hour later, at 400 ft., right over the front line, the engine suddenly began to shake itself out of the machine. I thought we had been hit (at last!), but actually a connecting rod had crystallized and snapped in half, quite enough to pack up a rotary engine.

It was an awkward situation in which to turn into a glider: but at 400 ft. there is no time to hum and ha—you have to find somewhere to put down. The difficulty about this was that the whole area was blasted by the bombardment— a contiguous area of shell holes most unsuitable for aircraft landings. But then, there, right underneath was a minute and miraculous pocket handkerchief of light green! How to get the Parasol down on that? I dived at it vertically, switching off and turning the petrol off as we fell, hoping to avoid fire when we turned over. At 50 ft. it was clear why the green patch was still green, it was a slope as steep as the roof of a house! We were rushing at it, zooming grandly up the hillside. Steeper grew the slope and I pulled the stick back and back till the Parasol fluttered into that green patch like a rook into a furrow. It didn't run 10 ft. and there we were! Intact! And pretty well in the front line! It was about as near to a miracle as any ordinary chap can get. We leapt out and jumped for a trench, expecting to be an immediate target for enemy gun fire. In fact two shells whooshed over missing the old Parasol nicely, then they seemed to lose interest and gave it up. Later that day my corporal rigger came out with a trailer and a rescue party. Somehow or other they got the wings off and hauled the fuselage back to the road. By evening it was all together again and I flight tested it in the dusk, ready for patrol next day.

9

Morane Biplane

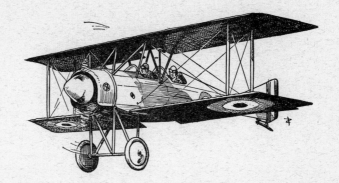

NUMBER THREE SQUADRON on the Somme was equipped with two flights of Morane Parasols and one flight of Biplanes. While the Biplane was unmistakably from the same stable as the Parasol, in a curious way the design had not come off. The Biplane had a 110-h.p. Le Rhône engine—not so sweet as the 80-h.p. engines in the Parasols which ran like sewing machines—and our admiration of the Biplane was chiefly because it was, for those days, quite fast. It flew level at 95 m.p.h., which was 10 m.p.h. faster than the Parasol.

Both in the air and on the ground this aeroplane had a somewhat waspish appearance. It looked dangerous and short-tempered and, though I cannot support this with any figures, I have a feeling that the extra speed made it pretty well invulnerable to enemy attack in the air. I do not remember any casualties in the Biplane flight. The aircraft had the same undercarriage and the same extraordinary tail as the Parasol. For artillery observation it was less satisfactory than the Parasol because of the lower wings which inevitably impeded the pilot's downward view.

The steps by which design advances have always held a fascination for me. Why was it that aircraft took so long to change over from the trussed box of the biplane to the self-supporting monoplane wing we know today? Of course the biplane was relatively simple to construct in such a way that it could withstand the strains of flight. All early aircraft were made of wood: the wings themselves were quite a work of art. The leading and trailing spars (made of straight-grained spruce) were carefully held apart by ribs which were shaped to the section of the wing. Broadly speaking the 'aerofoil' section was that of a bird's wing, slightly hollowed on the underside, where the leading edge tipped downwards and mounted on the aircraft slightly inclined to the line of flight. The forward speed caused the air to press against the lower side of the wing and so lift the aeroplane off the ground. This was the theory. It was some considerable time before experiments proved that two-thirds of the lift came from suction on the *upper* side of the plane and only one-third from beneath it. All these early wing sections were very thin. They were not more than three inches thick and the trailing edge was beautifully feathered off to nothing. But in the thinness of the section lay its weakness: it could never stand up to the speeds and strains of flight unless it were efficiently braced—hence the biplane.

It took many years, but gradually as more effort began to be concentrated on aircraft design and as wind tunnels began to show up what actually happened in the air, it became clear that wings could be thickened up very considerably without losing their efficiency or their lift—particularly as engine powers and speeds increased. We are still a long way from the miraculous construction of a bird's wing with its ability to vary its area and angle of incidence at will, to say nothing of folding up neatly on landing. But once designers had tumbled to the idea of cantilever construction of wing spars and the enormous strength which can be added to wing structure by covering it with a more or less rigid skin, the biplane disappeared into limbo and the evolution of 'clean' streamlined aircraft began.

10

Morane Scout

Iᴺ ɴɪɴᴇᴛᴇᴇɴ sɪxᴛᴇᴇɴ the Morane Scout was the 'cleanest' aircraft in service. Although the wings had the usual thin section used in those days and were braced with wires from kingposts above and below, the wing roots were faired into a 'monocoque' fuselage and the propeller had a conical fairing which streamlined the whole engine very neatly. In fact the Morane Scout was also often called 'The Bullet'.

That summer most pilots working up and down the Somme area on artillery observation or photography were haunted by the fear of being attacked by a Fokker. Nobody had ever seen one except head-on as it came in to fire. It had become such a bogey that when a German ferry pilot made the classic mistake (which British ferry pilots also made) of flying right over the lines and landing the other side, we were all delighted. The captured Fokker was taken to the aircraft depot at St. Omer and before 'Boom' Trenchard and all the big brass the Fokker was put up against the Morane Bullet, to see which had the better performance. To our delight it turned out that the Fokker's performance was in no way exceptional and that the Morane had a better climb and could turn inside the enemy. So the bogey was laid.

However, the Hun were ahead of us that year in one thing—they already had a machine-gun firing through the propeller. This made an enormous difference.

We had only one 'pusher' Scout, the D.H. 2, which could fire and attack head-on. Any other attack had to be from the flank or actually running away! On more than one occasion I went out with my observer Hun baiting; but in order to shoot the enemy down we had to turn tail and run! A ridiculous state of affairs.

In 1916 there were no 'scout' squadrons composed entirely of fighters; each squadron had one or two scouts attached to it, surplus to establishment, and certain pilots were allowed, more or less as a reward for good work, to take them up and go about looking for trouble. Nothing was organized and if the pilot was lucky and brought down a Hun, it was 'on the side' so to speak.

We had, I think, two Morane Bullets surplus to establishment. It was a very small aeroplane, so small that nobody above five feet six inches could get into it, but still that year it was the only aircraft which could fire through its propeller. We had not developed a gear which stopped the gun firing as the blades went past; but Moranes had fitted, on the back of the propeller, a deflector, made of hardened steel and shaped like a rain gutter. Any bullet that would have struck the propeller struck this deflector instead. This device, though it saved the blades, much reduced the efficiency of the propeller.

I once had the experience of what can happen to a propeller if the gear is not properly synchronized. One day in 1917 on patrol in my S.E. 5, I was testing my guns, when suddenly the machine began to vibrate in a quite frightening manner. It was evidently the engine and to stop it shaking itself to pieces I pulled up into a stall. As the propeller speed slowed down, I saw that one of the blades was not there! It was really quite a moment. The gun had literally 'fired through the propeller' and severed the blade at the root! Luckily I had plenty of height and was able to reach the emergency landing ground with a dead engine.

11

Bristol Fighter

I SUPPOSE THAT coming through seven months of the Somme on Moranes unscathed must have been responsible for my posting to the Testing Squadron in the autumn of 1916. Anyway when, after seven months of leaning out of draughty cockpits, I got acute conjunctivitis, I was sent home and posted to Upavon in November, 1916.

It was really a wonderful break. The alternatives—flying B.E. 2c's round the sky in search of non-existent Zeppelins, or teaching other people to fly—both left me cold. But the Testing Squadron, which vetted all aircraft offered to the R.F.C., was just the job. The design and appearance of the aeroplanes, the way they handled, their suitability for various duties, the grouping of the instruments, the cockpit comfort, the areas of vision; all these things fascinated me. I had ample opportunity to indulge them at the Testing Squadron.

Upavon is a bleak, windswept and inhospitable place. When I returned there for advanced training in 1942, 26 years later, it hadn't changed much. The orderly room, the roads, the take-off areas were all the same as in 1916. I almost expected to find the old aircraft in the sheds.

The Testing Squadron in those days was, as you may imagine, a rather immature and tentative outfit. Good 'general practice' in construction was far from established—indeed some new aeroplanes were dangerous just to fly round on circuits and bumps and would have broken up at once in a dive. But it was obviously necessary to have a clearing house for the dozens of new types (and modifications of old types) that were being offered to the R.F.C. The aircraft industry, under the immense pressure and stimulus of the war, was expanding and progressing at a great rate. Just to tabulate rates of climb and speeds at various heights was valuable; and to have test pilots who had experience of active fighting conditions gave quite a new slant to mere performance, for these pilots put premiums on handling, on manoeuvrability, on aerobatics, on 'terminal velocity' dives and so on—all of which characteristics demanded quite different constructional strengths from mere speed and climb.

When I reported for duty my new Flight Commander Captain Mayo in his little makeshift office in the sheds, greeted me cheerfully. He gave me the impression of being a very refined and sensitive man. Face, nose and lips were thin; so were his hands. He had none of the full-blooded fighting pilot's dash and smash: on the contrary, he seemed to view the qualities and defects of aeroplanes with the interested detachment of a scientist. (He became, in fact, a first-class designer in his own right after the war.)

The first aircraft he introduced me to was the Bristol Fighter. It was a prototype, the very first, original aircraft that was to become famous in the First World War, and at a glance—running a pilot's eye over it like a horsecoper—I knew it was 'right'. With its Rolls-Royce Falcon engine, it had a sturdy, businesslike air to it and looked as if it would take a lot of punishment. The pilot was, as usual, boxed in between the upper and lower planes, but the observer, behind him, had a ring mounting for his gun and a good arc of fire. Although the pilot had his own gun, firing through the prop by virtue of the famous Constantinesco gear, he could easily be 'jumped' from above because nearly the whole of the upper sky was blind to him.

'How about taking out the centre-section?' suggested my new Flight Commander. 'Then the pilot could see up.' To remove a bit of the wings, particularly the middle bit, right in the slipstream of the prop, would surely be taking away a lot of lift?

'Well, yes. But I think she'll stand it and it certainly would improve the view.'

'Let me take it up first.'

After the Morane, the Bristol Fighter was comparatively heavy and slow on the controls; but it was well co-ordinated and gave the pilot confidence. This aeroplane would not let you down. But when we got the centre-section out it was very different. The sudden gap in the top plane made me feel naked, as if I was being spied on, though the view was certainly much better. But how would it behave?

Take off, climb, flying level—all these seemed fairly normal. Perhaps the lack of that central hunk of lift made her a bit slow, but nothing much. However, on throttling back to glide, it was a very different matter. Here the difference in lift was at once noticeable. You had to put the nose right down to maintain speed. She dropped like a brick. Approach and landing were hazardous owing to a wide variety in attitude with engine on or off. It wasn't, I suppose, really dangerous; but it was no aeroplane for general use. Better to accept a poor pilot view than upset the general excellent handling. So we put the centre-section back.

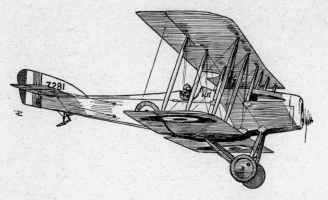

12

Martinsyde
Elephant

DURING THE FIRST TWO YEARS of the war the value of the Air Arm had been proved. At the outset the aeroplane was really a primitive mechanism; but the internal combustion engine, on which everything depended, made astonishing advances and by 1916 it was already as reliable as engines in lorries and cars. To start with 30 h.p. or 40 h.p. seemed a lot, but within a year the size of the power units had doubled and by the winter of 1916 engines developing 150 h.p. to 200 h.p. were already beginning to come off the production lines.

The horizon grew wider, aircraft could be bigger, they could fly faster and further. Their duties multiplied. They were still only ancillary to the ground forces, but they were beginning to develop definite tactics of their own.

Although 'total' war had not developed in 1914–18, the seeds of the pattern which was to be followed 25 years later could already be seen. Long-range reconnaissance, to find out the build-up of Hun factories, etc., and long-range bombing to destroy these installations, began to be a possibility. But to do this, new types of aircraft had to be evolved. They had to be able to fly high, they had to have a good speed, to make it difficult for enemy fighters to maintain a sustained attack, and they had to have range to penetrate into enemy country. All this, which now appears elementary and obvious, was new thinking in 1916. New thinking which sprang partly from the vision of the Chiefs of Staff and partly from the technical possibilities which crackled away in the heads of those early back-room boys.

The first aircraft of this new type that I flew was the Martinsyde. It was really like a rather cumbersome two-seater which had been made into a single-seater. The spare space had been filled with petrol tanks. Somehow adaptations of this kind never worked. The first example of it that I met was the B.E. 12— and that was an absolute cow. The Martinsyde was little better. But it had a splendidly reliable 160-h.p. Beardmore water-cooled engine with the big radiator behind the engine just like an old Renault car, and way down behind the wings, about 15 ft. away, was the pilot's seat. The pilot had an excellent view both up and down, but the Martinsyde was one of those curiously woolley aeroplanes that a pilot can never get hold of. It seemed to take a long time to accelerate and get off and it had a phenomenal 'float' when you flattened out to land, before the wheels had actually touched. Owing to the way the weight was slung out along the fuselage, engine, tanks and pilot, it had a very poor turning circle. Only aeroplanes with the weight concentrated were really manoeuvrable. On the other hand, it could carry two racks of 20-lb. bombs and had an endurance of about five hours, and it was for this long-range work it had been designed.

Although the Martinsyde Elephant saw service in several theatres of war (only No. 27 Squadron was completely equipped to operate them on the Western Front in 1916), it was soon taken out of service in France owing to a high casualty rate. Attacked by enemy fighters they were so clumsy and un-manoeuvrable they could not get away. Having no gunner they could not defend their tails. They were just sitting ducks, Albatros fodder.

Early 1917 saw another great change in the appearance of aircraft: camouflage. All through the Somme Battle my Morane was a white aeroplane, the natural Irish linen that covered the wings and the clear dope resulting in a warm cream finish, against which the red, white and blue roundels stood out clearly. But as soon as aerial attack became more common, it was clear that from above a white aeroplane would stand out clearly against the browns and greens of the earth.

The Martinsyde at Upavon is the last white aircraft I remember during the war. Soon after that all upper surfaces were doped chocolate colour. Later this was also variegated to include patches of olive green. It certainly did make aeroplanes less visible, but some disadvantage to the Allies remained—their red, white and blue roundels showed up more clearly than the black crosses of the enemy.

SOPWITH TRIPLANE

13

Sopwith Triplane

FIGURES AND FACTS, the inexorable data of wind tunnels, test beds, slide rules and practical experience have so narrowed down aircraft design that today it is difficult to tell one aircraft from another. But in 1917 even the production line was an experiment and few could even have guessed what direction design would take. We might wish to emulate the birds; but nobody then knew how to build a self-supporting wing strong enough to stand the strains of flight.

On the other hand practical experience on active service was beginning to point the way to obvious principles—a short ship turns quicker and in a tighter circle than a long one; however 'offensive' your aircraft, they still need to evade; pilots may be expendable, but they cost money to train, so don't throw their lives away by giving them poor machines.

What the pilots wanted was something that could dive like a swallow and change direction like a bat. In a dogfight manoeuvrability counted more than speed. It was up to the designer to meet the service requirement.

Way back in 1893 Horatio Phillips designed a multiplane and actually built a full-sized machine with a steam engine in 1904. It looked like a flying venetian blind, and although it never flew it sowed the idea of 'multiplaned' aircraft in people's minds. Before the war A. V. Roe had produced a sort of double four-winged box kite, and from these antecedents in 1916 sprung the Sopwith Triplane.

It was a little beauty. The rotary engine, tank and pilot were all bunched close together, so it could turn sideways or head over heels like a tumbler pigeon. Its three mainplanes carried all the area necessary for the load in such a small span that you could throw the Triplane from side to side like a leaf. Being from the Sopwith stable, all the controls were nicely balanced and the machine handled like a polo pony. The 'Tripe' vies with the Pup for pride of place in my heart for sheer flying pleasure. Both of them were underpowered and never had the success the designs merited in service for this reason. It was only with the Camel that Sopwiths finally scored a winner.

The Triplane had one weakness, it couldn't really dive; and, it was alleged, the wings came off if it was pointed at the ground with the engine full on. But nobody, as far as I know, had tried this to the limit. Having no parachutes it would have meant certain death and test pilots, though intrepid, were not quite as daft as that. So the 'Tripehound' (as it was affectionately called) never came into service with the R.F.C.

But in 1916-17 the Navy had its own air arm, parallel with that 'owned' by the Army. The Royal Naval Air Service had been recruited from a lot of boating types and spent their time (we said) waffling about on hydroplanes and escorting their blessed battleships instead of joining in the war. The R.F.C. were quick off the mark in ordering Triplanes; but when they found that the R.N.A.S. had ordered Spads, as this machine seemed more suited to offensive operations in France, the two services did a swap. The R.F.C. took on the Spads and the R.N.A.S. were glad to have the Triplanes. By the spring of 1917 the R.N.A.S. had several Triplane squadrons in Flanders where, in our S.E. 5's, we were often jolly glad of their help in dogfights.

The Triplane had a 110-h.p. Clerget engine, a nice rotary job that could be throttled back like a stationary. It was so well balanced that it would fly hands off on the tail-trimmer, which other aircraft boasted they could do, but didn't.

It could do more than this: set the engine at three-quarter throttle and wind the tail well back and the Tripe would loop indefinitely. I once did 21 loops in a row! But it was not in stunts like this that the charm of this aeroplane lay. It was perhaps the first really well-mannered and docile aircraft that responded immediately to the lightest pressure on the controls. Equipped with a single Vickers gun firing through the prop it proved a formidable adversary in a dogfight. Owing to the narrow chord of the three wings the pilot's view was almost good and throwing the aircraft from side to side was the work of a second to see under one wing or the other. Altogether the naval types did pretty well with the Tripe over France in 1917.

14

D.H. 4

THE FIRST FIGHTING SCOUT to be used in squadrons by the R.F.C. was a belligerent, efficient little pusher called the D.H. 2 (de Havilland 2). The pilot sat in a shoe well out ahead of the biplane wings, a 100-h.p. Monosoupape provided the power, and four metal longerons tied wings to tail. The D.H. 2 pilot could see everything (except his own tail). His gun needed no synchronizing gear. He handled a strong, manoeuvrable, aggressive little aeroplane, formidable in a fight and capable of giving a very good account of itself.

Although the D.H. 4 was nothing whatever like the D.H. 2 it came to us at the Testing Station bearing an already famous and respected name—a name which was to grow steadily more illustrious with the passage of years. From the pilot's point of view there was already something about the D.H. 4 that had style. I could not put my finger on it; it was just aesthetics.

The D.H. 4 was designed to do the jobs the B.E. 12 and Martinsyde had failed to do. In these it was highly successful owing to its well-designed observer's cockpit with its ring gun mounting which took care of attacking enemy scouts, and also thanks to its Rolls-Royce Eagle engine which gave it such a turn of speed that it could show a clean pair of heels to many of the Hun fighters.

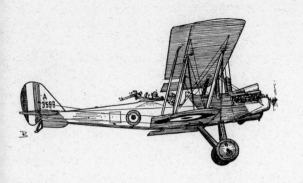

15

R.E. 8

H ow far should you carry free enterprise? Is it necessary to have 100 different types of cars, 20 vacuum cleaners, 50 cookers, 15 electric irons? Assuming they all do a fair job, the one that gets the majority of the market will be the one best advertised, whether it is really the best or not. In the end you pay more for the publicity than for the goods.

In 1917 there were five aeroplanes which were all designed to do the same job. All were biplane tractors, all carried a crew of two, all had the pilot in front and the observer and his ring mounting behind. There were differences in design details, of course; there were differences also in strength and performance. At Martlesham we could easily have eliminated four and concentrated production on one, while the four other firms went ahead with something else.

But free enterprise doesn't work like that, so we had the D.H. 4, the D.H. 9 (which grew out of the D.H. 4), the Bristol Fighter, the Sopwith 1½ Strutter and the R.E. 8.

The R.E. 8 was another product of the Royal Aircraft Factory at Farnborough. I don't know why, but even now something in me bristles at their designs! They were perfectly workmanlike, they did what was required of them, they were in no way unreliable or dangerous—but they were absolutely devoid of any charm. Even the S.E. 5 as the R.A.F. turned it out was an abortion; it was the pilots of 56 Squadron who turned it into a practical fighter.

The R.E. 8 had R.A.F. written all over it. It was a logical development of the B.E. 2c line, but 'modernized', one year later, to have pilot in front and observer behind. With a larger engine (I remember the enormous four-bladed propeller), overhang on the top planes and a sensible tail assembly, the R.E. 8 was also 'inherently stable' and did, in fact, fly straight and level with little or no attention, once it had been properly trimmed.

In 1917 the R.F.C. was expanding rapidly and we, who had been a year on active service, considered ourselves veterans. I was a Morane pilot, a Testing Squadron pilot, and S.E. 5 pilot and this seemed to me then a sort of pedigree which gave me caste and immense superiority! So I (and I think most fighter pilots) rather looked down our noses at those poor types flopping around the sky on reconnaissance in old flying bedsteads like R.E. 8's. When you're 18 you can be a great fool. After all, I'd been doing the same job as theirs the year before and might have remembered it could be pretty tough. But of one thing I'm certain. If I had to do it again I'd sooner do it on a Morane Parasol than an R.E. 8!

S.E.5A

16

S.E. 5

WHEN I LEFT the Testing Squadron at Martlesham in the spring of 1917, it was to be posted to No. 56 Squadron then forming at London Colney. The Squadron was to be equipped with the latest product of the R.A.F., Farnborough, the S.E. 5.

The S.E. 5 had already been chosen to equip a complete fighting squadron for combat overseas without ever coming to the Testing Squadron at all! There must have been some smart lobbying going on behind the scenes. Rumour said it was the finest scout ever built and that 'Boom' Trenchard was relying on it to regain the supremacy of the skies from Richthofen and his famous 'circus' of red Albatroses.

But when we started ferrying these new machines back from Farnborough to London Colney we were soon a bit gloomy. The S.E. 5 was not a 'sweet' aeroplane to fly and the machine-gun mountings filled us with foreboding.

Why the S.E. 5 was not fitted with two Vickers guns firing through the propeller, nobody knows. In fact it had only one so fitted. The second gun was a Lewis, mounted above the upper plane so that its fire was clear of the propeller. This gun carried a double drum with 100 rounds of ammunition in it. When the drum was empty it had to be reloaded from spare drums down beside the pilot's seat in the cockpit. The reloading was the snag.

The gun was mounted on a quadrant, the lower end of which was secured to the 'greenhouse' (of which more later). When his ammunition was exhausted the pilot released a catch and taking hold of a handle at the back of the gun pulled it down the quadrant. This was not difficult as the wind pressure helped the gun to slide down. When it was right down the muzzle pointed straight up at the sky and the drum was within easy reach, but, as the machine was travelling at about 100 m.p.h., as soon as the pilot put his hand into the grip on top of the drum and released it, it flew back into his face like a soup plate in a gale. Having got the empty drum safely into the rack, he had then to select a full one and get this out into the gale and back onto the gun. This was quite bad enough in the middle of a dogfight when there were other things to think about; but the gun was no use until it had been pushed back up the quadrant and locked into position on the top plane. This last effort often proved impossible. The quadrant mounting was of machined aluminium and in spite of greasing it and doing everything possible to make the slide work easily, it often resisted all the attempts of the pilot to go back up that curve. From all this technicality you can see, I hope, that this was a typical Factory invention which could never have been devised by any pilot who had been in a dogfight.

But this, after all, only added to the pilot's difficulties in combat. There was another general hazard built into the S.E. 5. This was the famous 'greenhouse'. At the lower end of the gun quadrant right in front of the pilot's nose was a sort of inverted celluloid coal scuttle. It was supposed to be a windscreen and pointing ahead through the middle of it (and anchored to the top of the fuselage) was a long black tube—an Aldis telescopic sight. Needless to say the sheets of celluloid of which this 'greenhouse' was made were difficult to see through and subject to all kinds of distortion. In addition we knew that any small oil leak could mist up the whole thing and make it pretty well impossible to see forward at all. Finally the aluminium frame of the 'greenhouse' had a rough, blunt metal edge within a few inches of our faces. In a crash this would cut us up nicely.

There was nothing to be done about the guns. We had to accept the armament

48

provided and do the best we could with it; but we all struck at the 'greenhouse' and immediately started to make modifications. We finished up with a small Triplex adjustable windscreen (such as you see on racing cars) with a hole through the middle for the Aldis sight. This was sufficient to protect our faces from the cold and hardly interfered with the forward view at all. When we arrived in France the whole Squadron was out of action for a fortnight until these modifications were finished.

All the same, the S.E. 5 was a sturdy, well-built job. When we left for France it was fitted with a 150-h.p. Hispano-Suiza engine. With this engine its performance was about equal to the German Albatroses, against which it was matched. But later that year a high-compression engine of 180 h.p. came out and this was followed by one of 250 h.p. made under licence at Wolseleys. Although the bigger engine was a bit heavier, the performance was greatly improved and the ceiling higher—a thing of paramount importance in a scrap. By the autumn of 1917 the S.E. 5 was a formidable opponent for any German fighter.

In every other respect the machine was quite normal in its handling. It could be dived to terminal velocity without breaking up. It had no vices and would spin left or right without being difficult to pull out, as some other aircraft were. It was easy to land and had a broad, strong undercarriage. If only it had had a more efficient armament it could not have been bettered.

A fighting scout is an invitation to pilots to try their hand at aerobatics and it is interesting, in retrospect, to see how all the aerobatics of the First World War were, in fact, limited by the safety belt the pilot wore. This consisted of an eight-inch canvas band which was secured round the waist with a quick release clasp. There were no shoulder straps and, of course, no parachute. In such aerobatics as an 'Immelmann' turn, a loop or a flick roll the centrifugal force kept the pilot in his seat. The spectacular part of First World War aerobatics really lay in the fact that they were performed very near the ground. Dangerously so; many pilots were killed through making mistakes they had no room to get out of. The slow roll, the roll off the top and inverted flying—any of which man-oeuvres First World War pilots were capable of doing—were all unheard of because no pilot could 'hang on his straps'; he had no straps to hang on!

This is not a book about the fighting exploits of 56 Squadron and the remark-able record they established during the summer of 1917, flying the S.E. 5 against an enemy which certainly at that time was always superior in numbers. It was during these months that the first elementary rules of fighting in formation began to be worked out—though there was no radio telephone, everything had to be done by signs. Still, 1917 remains the year when the dogfight began to be part of the war and aerial supremacy an important part of the overall picture.

The S.E. 5 was probably the first fighting aircraft to be produced which was reliable enough and steady enough to stand up to the rough and tumble of 30 or 40 aircraft milling around trying to shoot each other down. In such conditions pilots do not think much about 'handling'. They are pretty rough on the controls. Slammed into a dive, yanked into climb, pulled hard round in a split-arse turn, the aircraft structure had to stand up to enormous and sudden strains. The S.E. 5 came through this ordeal triumphantly and justified the belief of the top brass that it would give the Allies the supremacy of the air that year. It did.

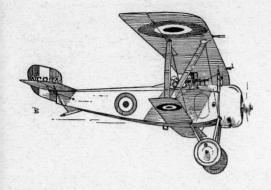

17

Nieuport
Scout

T HE FIGHTING ACES of the First World War, as I remember them, were
young men of high mettle and great energy. They seemed to burn. Perhaps
their metabolic rate was faster. Whatever it was, this extra energy, translated
into active service terms, meant they were always in the air. One aeroplane was
not enough for them. They got into scraps on pretty well every patrol and
often returned with a damaged engine or airframe. Their mood, on getting down,
was usually either one of frustration or fury and they would at once order out
another machine and take the air again to avenge a friend or get even with the
'one that got away'.

In the early days of 1917, Ball was the great Ace of No. 56 Squadron. While
Guynemer, the Ace of the Storks, had three Spads, Ball had only two aircraft
—his S.E. 5 and a Nieuport Scout. The handling characteristics of these two
aircraft were quite different, but Ball flew either of them, whichever was serviceable, without seemingly noticing the difference. He was a very 'uninteresting'
pilot. He never flew for pleasure and never indulged in any aerobatics. His aircraft was really nothing more to him than a flying gun-platform, something
to enable him to carry his machine-gun to the enemy and use it effectively.
This he did by his point-blank tactics, going right in, sometimes to within a
few yards of the enemy, without the least hesitation. On the other hand, he

was a very skilled and accurate pilot as the following incident will show.

One day we saw him coming in to land in his red-nosed S.E. 5. He had judged his approach a bit high and came in fast with a long float—very unlike his usual careful neat touchdown near the sheds. We looked at each other—was he losing his nerve, or something? When he taxied in the nose of the aircraft was covered with oil, so were his face and goggles. There were holes all round the cockpit and the elevator controls had been completely shot away! It was a shambles. However, somehow or other he had managed to extricate himself from the fight which had put him into a power spin. Centralizing everything he converted this into a power dive and from the dive back to normal flight *by winding back the tail trimmer*! Then he had flown his machine back to base on it. The trimmer was a device to alter the angle of incidence of the tail plane and so 'trim' the aircraft fore and aft so that it was neither nose or tail heavy. To use this trimmer as an elevator most of us would have said was impossible, the lag in response would have been too great; but somehow or other Ball had managed it. Characteristically he hardly spoke of it as we gathered round—for as soon as we saw the machine we knew that to get it back at all had called for quite exceptional coolness and skill. He turned away, called for his fitter to bring a rag to get the oil off his coat and helmet, walked over to the adjutant's hut to hand in his combat report and within half an hour was in the air again in his Nieuport.

The Nieuport Scout was a little aeroplane with a lot of personality. Like the Morane and the Spad it was a French design. It was powered by the big 110-h.p. Le Rhône engine and had a nice deep fuselage, very cosy to fly. But what made it instantaneously recognizable were the main planes. Technically it was a biplane; and there were certainly two wings one above the other. But, on close inspection, it turned out that most of the area was in the upper plane. This was quite large and overhung the lower one—which was, so to speak, atrophied, shrunk both in length and in chord (i.e. in width). From the pilot's point of view this arrangement had one great advantage; it meant a far better downward view. I find, writing these notes, that my mind constantly returns to this question of 'view'. It is a problem no contemporary pilot ever bothers about. But in those days, whether you wanted to see the ground below or enemy aircraft above, your eyeline was continually interfered with by the planes. Some aircraft seemed to be all blindspots and the pilot was constantly tilting and turning them to try to overcome his 'blindness'. It followed that any aircraft that gave us a better view had immediate appeal.

On that tragic evening of May 7th, 1917, when, after a classic dogfight starting at 14,000 ft. and finishing on the deck, only five of us got back to the airfield, Ball failed to return. Hope that he would turn up died in 48 hours. His effects were packed to be returned to his next-of-kin. I was detailed to fly his Nieuport back to No. 2 Aircraft Depot at Candas. It was a sad flight and the last time I ever flew a Nieuport.

18

Formation Flying

I SUPPOSE THAT in 1916 there was no formation flying because there were not enough aeroplanes about to fly in formation. By 1917 we had all begun to know what it was to fly in close to another plane—though it was very amateurish and rough compared with the sort of aerobatics R.A.F. exhibition formations can put up at Farnborough today.

We were learning. We used to practise in pairs and threes, always flying about 50 yds. apart. These were combat formations, loose and open to give room for sudden manoeuvres. We learned to use them in 1917 over the lines, where they soon proved their value. It was not until 1918 that we had time to spare for display formation flying. By this time I was with 61 Squadron at Rochford flying S.E. 5's on the defence of London.

A new flying officer had just been appointed to my flight. He was very young, raw, and thrusting—ham-fisted we use to call these new fellows who hadn't mastered the lightness of touch and deftness of movement which is the sign of a good scout pilot. He could do anything with the S.E.; but he yanked the machine about as if he was angry with it. It wasn't pretty to watch, and his riggers were always having to go over the machine, so much did he strain it. This wouldn't do. I told him off.

At this time all the squadrons in the brigade were preparing to compete in aerial fighting, formation flying, etc. We spent the days practising. I was in charge of squadron formation flying and when the new man came I thought it would be best to have him close to me, so I put him on my immediate left, with instructions that he was to stick there and fly soberly and quietly; thus would he best do himself and the flight credit. The formation made a lovely sight in the air. The boys were all up to their work, and the whole squadron turned and wheeled about the sky in perfect style. When it was over I fired a Very light and we came down and landed by flights. All except the newcomer. He had kept beautiful formation with me. I was very pleased with him. He was there all the time, his wings swaying slightly about 10 ft. off my tail. Nobody could have done better. The fellow could fly all right. Perhaps I had been a little hard on him.

I was standing on the tarmac, watching the last of the machines down, when the scream of an engine was heard. It was our youngster, to whom the repression of an hour's sober formation had been too much. He was diving, engine on, at the ground. He pulled out at about 10 ft. and zoomed up to 500 ft. or so on the momentum; but his pull into the zoom was rough and sudden, and his turn at the top was yanked, uneven. 'Gosh!' said one of the old hands, at my side, 'that's the way to pull your wings off.'

By now the machine had turned and was diving vertically, crazily, at the ground. Again he yanked out the machine with a terrible jerk, about 30 ft. up. It seemed to stagger. Then there was a tear, a wrench, and one pair of wings folded back. Bits of wood and canvas flew out. The machine fell headlong, struck the ground with a terrible crunch, and burst into flames. We rushed out —it wasn't a 100 yds. from the tarmac—to try and pull the man out. But the machine was an inferno. The flames crackled and roared up to a height of 50 ft. or more. It was useless.

The next day I went off on weekend leave, putting my deputy in charge. In the afternoon he took up the flight in formation.

We had two styles of formation flying: an open, fighting formation, in which the machines had at least 50 yds. between them; and a close exhibition formation, in which the closer the machines could fly the better.

In the close formation turns had to be made cautiously, else the machines might foul each other; but in the open we had invented an about turn, which reversed the direction quicker than going round in a half-circle. The leader did a half-roll on to his back, coming out directly underneath, facing in the opposite direction, while the two machines at either side of him turned left and right about respectively, crossing each other, and so regained their correct positions facing the other way. It was a neat manoeuvre, and the flight did it pretty well.

My deputy was a canny Scotsman; but he wasn't used to leading. He had the flight up in tight exhibition formation, and then must have lost his head, for he gave the signal for the about turn, and started his half-roll. The machine on his right, only about 10 ft. away, couldn't get out of the way. His propeller cut into the body of the leader, and the two machines, tangled up, spun down to earth. Both men were killed.

It was, I remember, one of those still mornings with high clouds massing when we carried them down under the flag. The age-old village church adjoined the aerodrome. The graves had been dug, and the Padre conducted the short ceremony at the graveside. The riggers had made crosses from four-bladed props, cutting off three blades short and leaving one long, and embossed their names on copper plates, covering the hubs where the bolts went through. We listened to those final simple words with, for my part, a sort of numbness, a feeling that this couldn't possibly have happened, that these men I had talked and joked with a day or two back were not really lying cold and mutilated in those damp holes, the earth crashing down on their coffins. The valedictory volleys cracked and echoed in the still beauty of the morning. The Last Post rang out and echoed away, as if calling up into that vault of blue; but the air that had borne them was as heedless as the earth that held them now. None but the few of us who knew them would remember or mourn. Well, we should all go that way. There was nothing to be done about it. I remembered the cynical war-time prayer: 'O God—if there is a God, save my soul—if I have a soul.'

These sudden stabs of tragedy punctuated the exuberance of the days: but did not stay long with us. There was a war on. People were apt to be killed in one way or another, and we were very young. We never thought for a moment that death could come to *us*. Death was something that happened to the other chap. Better so, for how could we have taken the risks we took with fear in our minds and hearts?

Indeed, looking back on it the risks we took were enormous and sometimes quite silly and unwarranted. The best example of these that I remember was one summer day at Hainault when the squadron indulged in formation flying of quite another kind. It happened this way.

The Mess President, on a visit to Stratford, had purchased a keg of old ale. When he got back with the spoils in a tender, it was just on lunch-time, so we all turned out to roll the barrel into the mess. The ale was broached and gushed out dark, mellow, and extremely intoxicating. The entire squadron voted it necessary to drink the mess president's health with two glasses apiece—and then one more for luck. Lunch became hilarious and finally rowdy. We were certainly not sober; but we were certainly not drunk: we were merely in excellent spirits. Then someone shouted, 'Let's go up for a flip!' Genius! We voted that Armstrong should head the snake, and took off—in all directions. My Flight Sergeant told me afterwards it was a hair-raising sight. Machines staggered into the air at stalling speed, missed each other by inches, turned vertically within a foot of the ground, invited every kind of accident; but somehow nothing happened, and at last we managed to get into line—a long snake of 18 machines. Having achieved this unique and beautiful formation, we came careering back over the aerodrome about 10 ft. up and set off contour-chasing all over Essex.

Of course we were crazy, but that was the mess president's fault. However, after half an hour's hedge-hopping and barn-skipping, the effects of the ale began to wear off, so that when Armstrong saw some duck over the Thames marshes and gave chase, the rest of us couldn't be bothered to follow him, and one by one we all came back and landed—one ginger-haired hero excepted.

On the tarmac we found the General Officer Commanding Home Defence and his A.D.C. talking to the squadron commander. Some questions of gun-targets or wind indicators took them out over the muddy aerodrome. It was here that Sandy spotted them. Whether he was anxious to show off his beautiful climbing turns, whether he resented people walking over the aerodrome were he wanted to land, or whether it was just Stratford ale and good spirits, heaven knows; but down he came like a hawk. The G.O.C. Home Defence was at first amused, screwing his monocle tighter into his eye; but soon he became alarmed, and finally sat, panic-stricken, in the mud while the undercarriage of the Camel shrieked by about a foot above his head and the slipstream from the prop blew his beautiful brass hat off. Now if you are a general, accustomed to the respect and deference of your subordinate officers, it is a little difficult to know how to deal with such a situation when sitting in the mud with a second lieutenant and a major on either side of you! This general replaced his hat and, making some quite unprintable remarks about the pilot, resumed his dignity. The three walked on.

But Sandy was not satisfied with this ignominious defeat of what (I presume) he thought to be three tommies wandering about the aerodrome, so he gave them the other barrel, as it were, and dived again. The result was precisely the same, except that the general managed to hold his hat on! By this time the seat of his trousers was sopping, his dignity had been outraged, and he was altogether a very angry general. It is a terrifying experience to be dived on by an aeroplane, particularly when the pilot is cutting it so fine; besides, there is always the chance he may miscalculate by a split second and cut off the heads of his target with the undercarriage. So the general was annoyed and intimidated. Sandy, zooming up to about 500 ft., half rolled on to his back, laughing like hell.

'I'll teach those ruddy A.M.s to go snooping about the aerodrome when I want to land,' he said to himself, and fell out of his half-loop into a third more gorgeous pounce. His objectives were still sitting angrily in the mud. This time he shaved them even closer than before, so that the general thought his hour had come and lay flat on his back cursing!

Meanwhile the rest of us were standing in groups on the tarmac, first on one leg, then on the other, divided between wild hilarity at the ridiculous figure cut by the general, and a fear of what would happen to that perfect idiot, Sandy, when he came down. Once the machine was safely on the ground with the engine off, the general retraced his steps, recovering indignation and composure at every stride. By the time he got back to the sheds all the pilots had mysteriously drifted away. The unfortunate Sandy was sent for by the major's office, and when we heard he had been deprived of his Sam Browne and put in irons for three days, the squadron was not in the least surprised.

His comment on returning to the mess was: 'Well, I bloody well put the wind up him, anyway!'

19

Spad

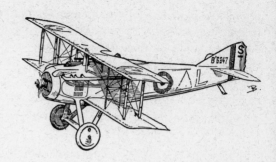

WHEN FIFTY-SIX SQUADRON had settled down—after the big tangle with the Richthofen 'circus' on May 7th when Ball was killed—it was necessary to show our aircraft to neighbouring squadrons up and down the front. Aircraft recognition was not taken as seriously then as it has been since, but at that time quite a number of new types of aircraft were appearing on both sides and pilots engaged in dogfights were not in the habit of taking chances. They would open fire at once on silhouettes they didn't recognize.

Nineteen seventeen was the first year in history when aerial combat became a recognized factor in warfare. Up till then aeroplanes had really only added a dimension to the war on the ground. They were, if you like, a moving hilltop from which to look over into enemy territory. Balloons had served the same purpose before. They enabled the commanders below to have intelligence of what was going on beyond their field of vision.

This obvious advantage was immediately countered by the enemy in three main ways. He could fire shells at the aircraft; if they were low enough down he could machine-gun them; best of all he could put up 'fighters' to shoot them down. It was in this way that the light, single-seater, offensive fighting scouts came into existence. Their business was to destroy the enemy reconnaissance aircraft. This naturally led to encounters with enemy fighter scouts on the same job. Soon both lots of fighters found that the best way to protect their own people was to shoot the enemy fighters out of the sky. Then their own reconnaissance could go forward unimpeded.

By 1917 this technique was recognized and fighters went out looking for other fighters. The supremacy of the air consisted in having an overall advantage so that machines engaged on reconnaissance or photography could get on with their job. Those who had the supremacy, having shot down the enemy fighters, would then harry his reconnaissance squadrons, shoot up his kite balloons and aerodromes and even take part in the land war by diving on ground forces and shooting up the enemy in their trenches.

One day in May, 1917, I was detailed to fly north in my S.E. 5 to an airfield near Dunkirk to show the aircraft to a new French squadron which had just come into our area. This squadron was commanded by the famous French Ace Guynemer. When I found the aerodrome and landed quite a selection of R.F.C. machines were there already. A general parade had been ordered so the French could familiarize themselves with their allies and not shoot us all down by mistake. Though I had heard of the Spad before, this was the first occasion when I had seen one at close quarters, for Guynemer's squadron—the famous Storks—was equipped with Spads.

The Spad was a very small, neat little aeroplane. It was a biplane, but the fuselage had been so much deepened that it almost filled the space between the upper and lower planes. Coupled with this it had a small propeller which enabled the undercarriage legs to be shorter and the general overall effect was one of stubby efficiency. Again it was no aircraft for a big man, though the fuselage was roomy once you were inside.

My great interest that afternoon was in Guynemer. He was a quiet, sallow boy, almost consumptive looking, but already famous throughout the French Air Force and the R.F.C. as he was accredited with over 50 German aircraft destroyed. That day he showed me, with some pride, his three personal aircraft. They were all Spads. One was a standard production type with its normal

Hispano-Suiza engine boosted to 180 h.p.; one was a slightly larger aircraft with a new 200-h.p. engine, and the last had a still larger engine with a geared down propeller. This enabled a pom-pom 'cannon' lying along the vee of the cylinder blocks to be fired through the hollow boss. This arrangement excited our admiration. Something heavier than a machine-gun with an explosive shell would give any pilot a great advantage in combat. I asked Guynemer what success he had had with his 'cannon'. He was very proud of it. His machine also carried a machine-gun loaded with tracer. A short burst to make sure he was on target and then the cannon for the kill. The pom-pom only carried about 20 shells.

I do not want to appear conceited, but at that time I was considered one of the best pilots in 56 Squadron, so when Guynemer challenged me to a mock combat over the airfield I accepted with alacrity. I knew our machines were fairly evenly matched and judged that my own flying skill would give me the edge over the Frenchman. But I soon found it was otherwise. Guynemer's little Spad was smaller and more manoeuvrable than the S.E. 5. He had a better climb and could turn in a smaller circle. The result was that as I sat in a vertical turn with the stick right back circling as tightly as the S.E. 5 could go, Guynemer just sat right on my tail turning in a slightly smaller circle so that he always kept his sights on me. Had I been an enemy, I should have been dead five times in the first minute. Do what I would, spin, half-roll, dive, climb, there he sat— just as if I had been towing him behind me. So I returned to the squadron that evening with a great respect for the Spad and for the boy who piloted it with such skill. Only a few weeks later, stalking an unsuspecting Hun two-seater with his cannon, Guynemer was just too much preoccupied, and an Albatros, coming down out of the morning sun, shot him out of the sky.

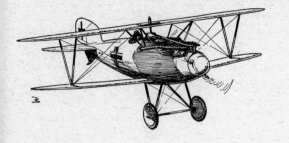

20

Albatros

T HE INTENSE INTEREST all wartime pilots displayed in their opponents
was natural. When we met the enemy high in the sky, we desperately wanted
to know what we were up against. Of course aircraft appear to vary a good
deal from the way they are handled. Not all pilots get the best out of their
machines, any more than drivers do out of their cars. But still to *know* that your
own machine is faster, climbs better and so on, is a most comforting reassurance
in those fateful moments before you engage.

But how could we get hold of these vital statistics about performance of
enemy aircraft? It was not easy. But sometimes an enemy pilot would be wounded
and be forced to land on our side of the lines; sometimes his aircraft, partly out
of control, would have to land and might be repairable; but more usually some
gormless ferry pilot who did not quite know where the lines were would cheerfully fly right over them and land on the other side. Then we got a new enemy
aeroplane intact—and so did the Hun when we did it.

It was in this way that one day we had a nice red Albatros delivered to us.
Having jubilantly painted out the black crosses and substituted our own roundels,
we were all encouraged to take it up.

While the body of the S.E. 5 had four longerons, braced like a wireless mast
and covered with fabric, already in 1917 the Germans were using a 'monocoque'

construction of moulded ply (far in advance of us) for the body of the Albatros. I don't know what it was made of; but it gave the impression of *papier mâché*. However, being rounded out like a fish, it was far more roomy and the whole machine seemed larger because of this cavernous cockpit. The engine, water-cooled, had a neat radiator in the centre-section, but was big and heavy. In fact the Germanic temperament showed up all along. The machine was sluggish, strong, reliable and determined. It had none of the feeling of lightness and grace that our aircraft had. Of course, every aeroplane has its own characteristics and very few pilots could take over the controls of a strange type and really measure up its capabilities in an hour or so. So it is probable we never really stretched it; but I am certain of one thing—to throw an Albatros about in the air was hard work and it would have made you sweat in a dogfight.

The best pilots are 'part' of their machines and we were always encouraged to be so at home with our aircraft that nothing could surprise us. Our reactions in an emergency would be 'second nature', instinctive, as if the aeroplane was an extension of our very self. So on summer evenings up for test (*never* on returning from patrol in case of unsuspected damage from enemy action) we would often climb up to play follow-my-leader or to fight mock duels among the clouds. It is one of the most thrilling of my memories.

Above were the towering majestic masses of the cumulus like fantastic pearls, their peaks turning pink with the approach of evening. Far, far below was the little earth already shadowed in the dusk. Climbing towards the sunlit radiance would be two young men, two small black specks, fighter aircraft, steadily roaring upwards on the biggest ski lift in the world.

From afar the cumulus had that solid enamelled look that groundlings know, but closer it became a series of savannahs of new snow, soft as swansdown, glistening with light. Ahead perhaps was a gorge, a steep vee of deep evening blue with cloudcliffs either side towering up and up high above our heads. Nose down, full out, we would charge this magical ravine, keeping just far enough above the clouds for them to retain their feeling of solidity. Steeper and steeper, faster and faster, grew the dive and then with a roar we were through the bottom and, stick hard back, pulling up and up and up over the rounded hills beyond till, losing speed, we paused to survey the immense snow fields again below us. Then selecting another cave, another valley or another cliff, we were off again. It was glorious. Power was there under the hand to command. Skill was there to fling the tiny aircraft like a swallow through the evening light. Something of poetry and youth must I think have crowned those hours and left us with memories of beauty and grandeur and freedom no other men can ever know. Our purpose to destroy was quite forgotten. The earth that bore us was so far below we had not to remember it. We lived like spirits in an airy loom striking great arabesques of flight across the weft of evening.

When it was over, side by side, eyeing each other through our goggles and close in the way people are who have shared a wonder, we would sink quietly back to earth, our engines just ticking over. Then at the airfield with a last flourish, throw the machines up and over, left and right and roll them in to pull up just before the sheds. At 19 who could ask more of life?

21

Sopwith Dolphin

T HE DOLPHIN was a 'back-staggered' scout, that is to say, a biplane in which the upper wing was set not square above the lower one, but somewhat behind it. The cockpit was so placed that the pilot's head came out just in front of this upper plane and on the same level, so he could look behind him over the tail. The back-staggering also gave him a fine forward and sideways view. Altogether, for a biplane, the Dolphin was about the best layout ever designed and it was a pity the machine never came into extensive use with the R.F.C.

I never flew the Dolphin and came in contact with it only once in curious circumstances which I shall always remember.

It was early summer of 1917 and the first of the new S.E. 5a's had been delivered to the squadron. This had an identical airframe, but was fitted with the new 250-h.p. Wolseley Viper engine which greatly improved its performance. At the time it was, as far as we knew, the fastest and finest fighter in the force.

The new machine was given to me to test. It was a beautiful afternoon and as our dogfights had been getting higher and higher—as both sides tried to gain the initial advantage of height in their attacks—I thought I would see what ceiling we should have with the new S.E. 5a. I climbed north away from the airfield towards Calais and soon saw the sweep of the Channel below me. Here I circled east towards Dunkirk and then turned in a big sweep right in over Kent and Sussex. By this time I was at 22,000 ft., England right below me. There was always something nostalgic about a return to Blighty. Even to be home five miles above ground was something, especially when you could see in the heavenly afternoon the smoke of woodfires and the green of English fields. Quite unsentimentally, with the stoicism of youth and the time, I wondered if I should ever walk them again.

Then as I came south, engine off, dropping slowly through the honeyed air of the warm day, I saw St. Omer far below. It had been my old stamping ground. There the year before Patrick, the chief test pilot had taught me to loop the B.E. 2c, to fly the Morane and had bawled me out when I turned the Bullet over. Why not land there for a cup of tea? Maybe Patrick was still there. I could show him the new bus. So I came down to about 5,000 ft. when my eye caught sight of a strange aircraft circling below me.

I dived at it, but did not recognize the type. Back-staggered wings—a stationary engine. Single-seater. All this I took in as I turned on to the stranger's tail. It was then he saw me and pulled into a tight vertical turn. So did I. But his was tighter and he gradually worked round. So I flick-rolled onto the other bank. So did he. Now he was neatly tucked in behind me—and I was a dead man. What were things coming to when a crack fighter pilot from a crack fighting squadron could be made a fool of by some tyro from an aircraft depot? This needed looking into. I dropped on to the deck. So did the Dolphin. When I walked over to greet my adversary—of course, you have guessed—it was Patrick, one of the finest pilots in the force. 'Hullo, Lewis,' he laughed. 'Still learning to fly?'

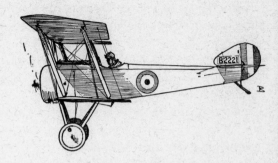

22

Sopwith Pup

O**F ALL THE AEROPLANES** of the First World War, by far the prettiest to look at and sweetest on the controls, was the Sopwith Pup.

I first saw what turned out to be the forerunner of the Pup at Brooklands in 1915. As trainee pilots, lumbering round the circuit in Longhorns, it seemed to our young eyes the most wonderful, beautiful aeroplane in the world. And when Hawker, the test pilot of Sopwiths, took it up and flew it stylishly round Brooklands, we were all enraptured. When, to cap it all, he flew the little thing *under* the Byfleet footbridge that spanned the banked track, we were Hawker fans for life.

This feat, which certainly needed accurate judgement and nerve, was not quite so amazing as it sounds. Our Longhorns had a 55-ft. span while the Hawker mount was under 25 ft. across. It was a tiny aircraft, too small for a tall man to get into. It had a seven-cylinder Gnôme engine that developed 50 h.p. and I can still see its little white biplane wings and neat little tail. It was all so beautifully proportioned, a worthy forerunner of the whole stable of Sopwith aircraft, which, right through the war—and since—were of such outstanding design. They filled the eye, they 'looked right', we used to say. A pilot knew beforehand when he took over a new type of Sopwith that it would handle like a thorough-bred.

I did not see a Pup at close quarters until 1918 when posted to Rochford to 61 Squadron Night Defence which had been equipped with Pups. Although the squadron was just changing over to S.E. 5's flight commanders managed to wangle one or two Pups surplus to establishment for joyriding.

In those two years the Pup had undergone some modifications to try to keep it operational. Mine was fitted with a 100-h.p. Mono and didn't handle so sweetly as the original with its 80-h.p. Le Rhône; but the Pup with any engine was just the job for those private 'flips' which, though quite unauthorized, were so much part of the flying life of those days.

In my Pup I used to fly 50 miles over to supper with friends in Suffolk, putting the bus down in a field near the house. After supper, in the summer twilight, my host would swing the prop and I would slip out through the elms after a 50-yd. take-off run and drop quietly back to Rochford sheds by dark. Also in the Pup I put down in a field where the Kingston by-pass now runs to walk up to Coombe Hill and spend the evening with Lily Elsie and Ivor Novello, both of them then at the height of their youth and beauty.

But not all the trips were 'roses', and I remember one particularly that was the sort of classic experience all pilots know. I had flown down to the Isle of Wight to see my father who had just been called up as an anti-aircraft gunner. After spending the day with him I left for home about 5 p.m.

It developed into an awful journey. A heavy bank of fog came up and forced me lower and lower, so that at last I gave it up and climbed clear above it to 8,000 ft., trusting my compass to get me back to Rochford. I hoped that over the east coast it might break, but I was out of luck. As far as I could see in every direction was an unbroken floor, yellowish in the setting sun. Up there it was all right, a clean dome of blue, full of pale sunlight; but this vast tranquillity did not reassure me. I didn't like the colour of that floor. It was not cloud, it was fog; and how the devil was I going to get down?

I flew on for a couple of hours. Petrol would be getting low. Better to come down while I had something in hand than to be forced down willy-nilly. I shut

F

off and dropped into the fog, watching the altimeter like a cat. Here I should point out (for the benefit of the uninitiated) that an altimeter is really a barometer. To set it at zero before you leave the ground there is a thumb-screw beside the dial. But the ground at Rochford was not necessarily at the same height as the ground I was at this moment dropping towards. I might come out over a hill, say 200 ft. higher than Rochford. My altimeter would still read 200 ft.—but I should hit the ground just the same. Forgetting this has accounted for many an accident.

I was not going to be caught if I could help it, but the trouble was that in a fog I should not see the ground until I was right on it. The needle dropped to 500 ft. I opened the throttle and dropped slowly, buzzing the engine on the button switch. If I suddenly saw a hill or a church spire, I should have full power to help me away. Now I forgot the altimeter and kept my eyes on the fog below me, peering through it anxiously for the first signs of the earth. Suddenly, an elm tree right ahead! Engine! I zoomed it, missing the crown by a few feet. It was one of a row, the edge of a field. Well, now I knew more or less where the ground was, anyway. I edged round slowly, looking at the stubble beneath me. How big was the field? Could I get down in it? Were there high trees all round? I peered anxiously. More trees, then a gap. If I could strike that gap, I might be able to get in. I circled away. Now everything was lost in the fog again. I must trust to my sense of direction and get down below the tree level—or I couldn't hope to get into the field. I dropped, flipping the engine anxiously. A tree ahead! I kicked the rudder and slid sideways, putting it on my right. Was there one to the left? Yes; but just room to squeeze through. Telegraph wires? Apparently not. The hedge passed underneath, the stubble was beneath me. She floated on for what seemed an eternity. At last I touched the ground. The opposite hedge loomed up. Should I stop in time? Should I run into it? The heavy stubble dragged at the wheels. The Pup came to rest nosing the hedge. Whew!

I jumped out. After the noisy engine, the sudden silence was profound. The world was holding its breath, suffocating under this dank blanket of vapour. The trees were dripping quietly, monotonously, as if weeping for the death of the world. No signs of human habitation. Not a sound broke the stillness. I pushed through the hedge, found a lane, and followed it to a large house. I rang the bell. 'Where am I?' I said.

The sudden apparition of a stranger in flying kit on such an evening must have startled the maid. She fetched her mistress. I was a few miles from Gravesend. So much for the compass course. I thought I was in Essex, I turned out to be in Kent. Well, what of it? I was down, anyway. Next morning the fog had cleared. The grocer's boy swung my prop, I squeezed out through the gap again, crossed the river, and made the aerodrome on the last drop of petrol in the gravity tank.

Still that Pup gave me one of my few moments of real terror in the air. I had been doing some aerobatics, 'stunts' as we called them then, and my engine had been off or perhaps the vapour got trapped under the cowling. Anyway when I released the button switch the nose of the aircraft was a flash of yellow flames and a horrible smell of burning rushed back over me. Fire! In far less time than I take to write this, I had the main switch off, the petrol off and the machine was in a sideslip to blow the flames out sideways away from my face. A second later the fire was out. I wasn't going to risk switching on again, so I brought her carefully down to the field as if I had a dead engine. Stupid, but I never quite trusted the beloved Pup again after that.

What a fascinating side of the human make-up lies in the way we 'associate'. I mean, how two totally irrelevant thoughts evoke each other. When we see one, we hear the other; when we feel one, we think the other and so on, indefinitely. I associate Arthur Rhys Davids with a passage from Keats, Beery Bowman with a vulgar story, 'Poor Butterfly' with a dance in Yeoman's Row—and the Sopwith Pup with castor oil.

Nor for the usual reasons. Rotary engines used castor oil as a lubricant. It was fed into the crankcase and flung out through the cylinder heads as the engine ran. All these engines used a great deal of oil. As it was flung out, it burned. And the bitter nutty tang of burnt castor oil is one of the most nostalgic memories of any

71

First World War pilot. He will remember the slow clonk, clonk, clonk as the mechanic 'sucked in', turning the heavy two-bladed propeller backwards. Then the quicker, clonkety-clonk, clonkety-clonk as he rocked the blade up and down getting ready for the pull that would start her. He remembers the man's shouted 'Contact!' and the pilot's fingers on the main switch *outside* the cockpit (for the mechanic to *see*, because pilots sometimes shouted 'Off!' when the switch was still on. I have known a mechanic cut to pieces by such a moment of forgetfulness). The pilot replies with a repeated 'Contact!' Then, with all his strength, the mechanic pulls down on the heavy blade against the engine compression, the engine fires, a cloud of blue smoke whirls backwards, flattening the blades of grass—and you, or I, or any of our breed standing behind, leaning forward, pressing against the slipstream, hearing the roaring engine, smell that never-to-be-forgotten smell of burning castor oil.

Nowadays oils have changed and only very occasionally do you get a sudden whiff of it. Then, in one breath, you leap back 50 years and stand leaning on the wind in the days of your youth.

SOPWITH CAMEL

23

Sopwith Camel

AFTER BEING WOUNDED and returning from France in the summer of 1917, I was posted to Hainault Farm, a Home Defence aerodrome just beyond Ilford. It was there I met the third 'important' aeroplane of my flying career in the First World War—the Sopwith Camel.

The Camel, so called because of a slightly 'humped' top line to the fuselage, was another single-seater biplane scout fitted with a rotary engine, the Clerget, developing 130-h.p. The pilot was hunched in behind the flat engine, the tanks were the full depth of the fuselage just behind the pilot—and all this meant the weight was highly concentrated and made for very lively handling characteristics. The Camel, in fact, was a beauty. It was sturdy enough to stand rough flying in a dogfight, handy enough to outmanoeuvre anything it came across. In addition it had two Vickers guns firing through the propeller and soon proved itself a very offensive weapon indeed. Beyond all this, it had all the Sopwith characteristics of viceless, well-balanced handling. It was light, responsive, comfortable and pilots loved it. Indeed it played an important part in maintaining Allied air supremacy right up to the end of the war.

The forward stagger of the main planes gave the pilot a good forward and downward view which served him well in a dogfight; but later, when the machine began to be used as a night fighter, to attack enemy bombers at home or overseas, the positions of pilot and tank were reversed. This brought the pilot out just aft of the main planes and gave him an excellent forward and upward view. Although we did not think the Camel handled quite as well with this arrangement, it was better suited to the job.

When I joined the squadron at Hainault, the defence of London wasn't a very serious affair. There had been one or two isolated daylight raids; but these had been at long intervals. Somehow or other the Hun knew we were ready for him and had the sense not to push his head into our mouths. We spent the time perfecting our formation flying, brushing up on aerobatics, and, since we were only half an hour by car from the West End, in frequent visits to town. It was a very good war while it lasted.

But, suddenly one September evening, we had news about dusk of a flight of German aeroplanes approaching the Thames Estuary, and in half an hour the whole character of Home Defence changed.

It is difficult for anyone today to understand such a situation. In 1917 night flying was unheard of. Apart from one or two heroes who went chasing Zeppelins in B.E.'s, nobody dreamed of going up at night. I had done several hundred hours in the air, but I had never flown at night. There was no night training. No cockpits were fitted with any instrument lighting. No dials were luminous. We were caught completely unawares.

It was just luck I happened to be in the Mess. Most of the chaps had already left for town. With one or two others we quickly togged up and got the machines out. We raided the stores for hand torches and climbed on board. We ran up the engines and checked the revs and oil pressure with the torch, flipped it off and put it back into our pockets—all the rest would have to be luck and airmanship.

I confess I was terrified. Though I don't remember a moment's hesitation in deciding to get up into the air and find the enemy if I could, I had a parallel stream of thought which told me emphatically that I had no lights, and that the night was as black as the inside of a cow. Once in the air I should be able to see nothing, and if I got down alive I should be damn lucky!

Somebody rigged up a line of flares, paraffin-soaked cotton waste burning in a bucket. A typical smoky smell always to be associated in my mind with that first night flight. I taxied out along the flare path, turned into wind, and with that mixture of trust and stoicism all pilots know, pushed open the throttle.

A second later I was reassured. Magically, lyrically reassured. For the dreaded blackness was a wonderful misty landscape in which the Thames Estuary, like a pool of silver, bisected the Kent and Essex coasts, every roof top reflected the radiance of the rising moon, the plume of smoke from an approaching train lay like an ostrich feather on the woods. An exquisite, silent, fairy-like world of mist and meadow was spread below me. No need to use the torch! I could hear my engine revs, feel my air speed and I knew my country.

So I continued on up to 14,000 ft., watching the probing searchlight beams, looking for Archie bursts to help me to locate the enemy and noting a few heavy red glows lower down from the heart of London where the bombs were bursting.

Inside my patrol line was a barrage of balloons—a deterrent against bombers (never as far as I know successful in catching a careless raider)—outside was a second line of balloons. So I stomped up and down in the corridor, like a scorpion in a sandwich, never on that occasion, or on dozens of other patrols during the next six months, seeing a sign of the enemy. One or two lucky men, like 'Flossie' Brand (one of our flight commanders) ran into Gothas and promptly shot them down. (Flossie went in so close that he singed his eyebrows when the Hun caught fire!) But generally our patrols were two-hour stretches of frustration, for although it appeared one could see for miles, the moving speck of an aircraft anything more than a 100 yds. away was invisible. All we could hope to do was locate the glow of an exhaust. Home Defence was a pretty slow business.

Reassuring on that first night were the golden pinpoints of the burning flares like rich brooches of light on the dark earth. Soon we could find our way all around the area by the pattern of these flares. That night I came down rather fast, anxious about the landing, determined not to stall short of the field. The air was clear down to 10 ft., then, suddenly, I was in a thick white blanket of mist. The flares came up through it, bursting on me as I passed them. It was eerie and anxious, but quickly came the reaction 'I must be almost on the deck'. I cut the engine, held her off and a moment later the wheels rumbled. All was well!

Back in France a year later the golden brooch of flares had gone because the German night bombers found it an attractive target for their eggs. We were forced to use a trolley about six feet long fitted with three Aldis lamps. On returning to the airfield, the pilot gave his call sign by flashing the recognition light on the belly of the aircraft, the trolley turned on the lights, the aircraft landed in their beam and the lights went off immediately.

It wasn't much to land by and France without flares was quite easy to get lost in. The new flashing beacons that should have served to give us our bearings were new and strange. So one of my pilots, quite lost, his petrol running low at the end of a two-hour patrol, was delighted to see the beams of the Aldis landing trolley below him. He came down, undershot, went round again and landed— on a road, in the beam of car headlights, 150 miles from home!

Although it is nothing, strictly speaking, to do with the handling of aircraft, there is a final episode on the Camel which, in retrospect, is so striking, that I cannot resist including it.

Next year, 1918, I was still on Home Defence and stationed at Rochford just outside Southend. One day the wireless officer came up to me and asked me if I would help him try out a new gadget that had been sent down by the Air Ministry for test. Now a wireless officer in a fighting squadron was, in those days, practically surplus to establishment. He had virtually nothing to do since none of the aircraft had any wireless equipment whatever. However, he was a nice sandy-haired lad and I asked him what his gadget might be. He explained he had a little black box he wanted to fit into my cockpit into which I could plug a pair of earphones. Then I would go up and cruise round the aerodrome and he would *speak to me* from the ground! I was to tell him when I came down whether

I had heard him. I objected that the earphones would mean cutting a hole in my helmet and I had no intention of doing that. He produced a new (and very ill-fitting) helmet with earphones in it. So, rather reluctantly, I agreed. I got up, circled round as arranged and I did hear something rather indistinct in the headphones and even a bit of a gramophone record. Next day he proposed we reverse it. I could take what he called the transmitter up into the air. Then I would speak to him and he would try to hear me. This also we managed, or at least he said he had heard me.

This was the first time I came into contact with sound broadcasting. It is the only test of this kind that I have ever heard of. It took place several years before the British Broadcasting Company was formed. I was, as it turned out, to be one of the founder members of that organization; but—and the interest lies purely in this—all the implications of the experiment passed right over my head! I saw nothing of particular interest in it, and if anyone had said this was the beginning of a mass communication that would change society, I—well, what would you say to a man today who told you he would be spending next Easter on Venus?

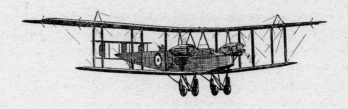

24

Handley Page

I FIRST SAW a Handley Page on Rochford Aerodrome in the summer of 1918. To single-seater 'scout' pilots it looked huge, and we certainly felt about it as the Bedouin did when they first saw it in Arabia: 'Surely this is the sire of all aeroplanes from which the rest have foaled.'

Handley Page is now a famous name in aircraft design: in 1918 it was relatively unknown. But the firm had produced the first big, twin-engined, long-range bomber and its effect was felt by the enemy when the R.A.F. raids began to get into their attack in 1918.

We live in an age of specialization. People know more and more about less and less. Soon we shall know everything about nothing and nothing about everything. In 1918 bomber pilots, fighter pilots, single-engine pilots, twin-engine pilots and so forth, did not exist. There were simply pilots: period. A lot of this *mystique* is nonsense and every emergency proves that people can learn all sorts of things and cope with all sorts of difficulties if the need arises and they are given the chance. Anyhow there stood the Handley Page which had to be taken, as far as I remember, to some airfield up in the Wash, and there stood I.

Climbing up into the machine was like setting out for an ascent of the Matterhorn, but, once up, there was a fine view and you could *walk about* in the thing! Whoever heard of an aeroplane as big as that! And with two engines you could actually *steer* by opening one up more than the other! True, it was like a lorry in the air. When you decided to turn left, you pushed over the controls, went and had a cup of tea and came back to find the turn just starting; but it had a nice comfortable, big car feeling, leisurely and relaxed. If you had to drop bombs about the place, well, this was a gentlemanly way of doing it. As for *flying* the thing, you couldn't really call it flying, after scouts. And if anyone had told me I was not a twin-engine pilot and would need a proper course and some dual before being *allowed* to take the thing up . . . I can't imagine what I should have said. I suppose I should have asked when he was certified.

25

Vickers Vimy

COMPARED WITH THE HANDLEY PAGE the Vimy was a small compact aeroplane. Throughout the war Vickers had not had much success with their own designs and the Vimy was produced late in 1918 and never, I think, became fully operational. It was, for those days, a large aeroplane, a biplane, a twin; but there was a certain businesslike practical air about it. The Rolls-Royce engines were steady and reliable, the controls effective and positive; flying the machine one had a feeling of immediate response, accuracy and docility.

It was 1919 and the vogue for long-distance flights was just starting. I had already been in the Vickers civil aviation department for a year. Whether Vickers suggested an Atlantic flight to Alcock and Brown or whether they proposed it to Vickers I cannot remember; but suddenly (it seems now) they were there in the office, on the corner of Sloane Street and Knightsbridge, and a lot of work was being done on petrol consumption and long-range tanks for the Vimy. I had nothing to do with the preparations for the flight except to fetch the aeroplane from an aircraft park (where new aircraft were stored) somewhere on Salisbury Plain and bring it back to Brooklands. There it was stripped out and the long-range tanks fitted.

All the details of that remarkable flight are too well known to be repeated here. The Vimy was given to the nation and stands in the Science Museum,

VICKERS VIMY

South Kensington. When I see it there I like to recall I was the first to fly it, even if only for 40 minutes.

Later that year Quentin Brand made the first flight to South Africa (for which he was knighted). Again I was detailed to fetch the new aircraft from the Park at Hendon and bring it across to Brooklands. I have reason to remember that flight very well.

In those days engine-driven petrol pumps did not exist. The main tanks had petrol pumped from them to a gravity tank (on the top plane) by means of small reciprocating pumps driven by diminutive wooden propellers. The speed of the aeroplane spun the propeller, turned the pump and kept the gravity tanks full. Simple—as long as the pump worked. Clipped on the side of one of the struts near the pilot's seat was the rubber feed pipe by which the petrol passed from the fuselage tanks up to the gravity tanks. Half-way up the strut the pipe was cut and a small visual gauge inserted. This consisted of a window—about the size of a penny—with a bit of reeded prismatic glass in it. When the petrol was flowing properly there was no refraction, and the gauge showed black. When the petrol ceased to flow, it showed white. You can see the gauge on the Transatlantic Vimy at the Science Museum.

When I arrived at Hendon that day, it was blowing a gale. I checked the aircraft, ran up the engines, turned into wind, opened up and was airborne in 50 yds., so strong was the wind. Once aloft I turned south for Brooklands, climbing over London. Checking instruments, I looked at the tell-tale petrol gauge. It showed white. The pump had packed up. There was fuel for 20 minutes in the gravity tank. What to do? I had the flash that all pilots know—engines cut, houses below, crash landing, fire, sudden death, the lot.

Then I remembered the emergency petrol pump. It was a sort of large stirrup pump and had been placed, God knows why, in a practically inaccessible position behind the left hand side of the pilot's seat. To reach it the pilot had to half turn and grasp the pump handle behind and below his shoulder and pull it *upwards*. As a refinement to the torture, the pump only worked on the *up* stroke.

I was alone in the aeroplane, the two Rolls-Royce engines were eating up the petrol, the weather was so rough the machine was wallowing all over the sky. I throttled back, fought the gale, flying with my right hand—the machine was big and quite heavy—and with my left hand started to pump. The gauge soon showed black. Hurrah! The hand pump was doing its job. But very soon the muscles in my shoulder began to start aching. The pulling action was awkward, the pump could not have been more stupidly placed. But I dared not stop, for if the engines once cut, there was no hope of putting down in the maze of houses and streets. It grew into a sort of nightmare. My shoulder grew numb. I could not pump anymore. I *had* to go on pumping. If ever a pilot was glad to see his destination I was glad to see Brooklands. I put her down, taxied in and just sat there, exhausted, till the mechanics climbed up to see what on earth I was doing. I made some highly-coloured remarks relative to the pump. I hope 'Flossie' Brand, as we called him, never had to use it on his way to the Cape.

Tailpiece

THERE IS AN EXPERIENCE that every pilot knows. It is a dreadful day, low clouds and rain, and when he takes off the pattern of trees and woods and fields is a dark, depressing tapestry of grey and blacks. The ceiling is down to perhaps 1,500 ft. He has hardly time to check his instruments and course before the clouds envelop him. In a second the sombre earth is gone and around him is a featureless cloak of vapour with no horizon, no top, bottom or sides to it. He is suddenly alone, in nothing! Settling down onto instruments he climbs steadily through it, knowing there must be a top, but ignorant of how high above him it may be. The clouds seem to come right into the cockpit, pressing in on him and there is nothing but the roar of the engine and the pointers on the dials. It is oppressive and sometimes terrifying, for curiously enough it requires courage for a pilot to trust his instruments. He feels the aircraft is slipping this way or that, it is turning, stalling, diving. But he knows he must suppress his own instincts and keep everything straight and steady. The bumps throw him about, the aircraft shudders. In the early days before we had reliable instruments I have often sweated in these conditions, particularly with the compasses fitted to the early Camels, which, at some speeds, spun slowly round and round like a top! If he panics, he may fall out of the nightmare in a spin; but, if all goes well, the clouds suddenly turn golden, the blue appears and a moment later he is through!

Through into another world of unimaginable serenity and clarity. The terrible clouds have turned to a level pavement of virgin snow, the heavens are a miraculous vault of blue, crystalline, dazzling and perfect. Such a fantastic change makes a man want to shout and sing at the glory of it. The sun shines. The shadows of the struts are on the wings. The warmth and light permeate his body. He is alone with the wonder. No other breed but his own can share these things that he has seen and known.

So were the first days after the Armistice, days of peace, extraordinary, unimaginable. All the hopeless, futile terror of it had gone and there, ahead, lay life! We had come through! We were alive!

All that is now 50 years ago and once again since then the ideals for which men fight have turned sour and meaningless. War, like an earthquake, twice in my lifetime, has shaken everything we valued to pieces and settled the crust a little more tightly and inexorably round our hearts. There is something relentless and chilling about the march of events. We tremble at the tread of that thousand-headed monster we ourselves have created.

For centuries the fastest thing on earth was a galloping horse. Then, speed became our god and soon, with radio, changed the whole face of civilization. But what is the effect on man? There are strange things, strange fatigues that air-crew (and passengers) know, strange lethargies and after effects which may be no more than the consequences projecting the human organism through the magnetic field of the earth at speeds for which it was never designed.

Looking back with a certain nostalgia on the days of my youth, what we seem to be losing, at an alarming rate, is our area of 'free manoeuvre'. The margins of life were wider when I was young. Men were on their own. They met their decisions, their crises, their battles unaided and inevitably grew in stature because of it. Would Nelson have fought Trafalgar or Gordon perished at Khartoum if airlifts and radio communication had existed?

We pilots of the First World War were the last to enter the age-long lists of single-handed combat. Alone, without parachute or radio, we fought our own fight high in the sky like champions before the eyes of the armies beneath. There we won, or lost, lived or died, by our own skill and courage—and no Big Brother breathed down our necks and told us what to do.